women

writers

talk

dedication

To these novelists, for their writing, which has intrigued, absorbed and consoled me, and for their generosity in interview. And to the librarians of Morley College, for their willingness and help and support to the desperate student and writer.

women

writers

talk

Interviews with

10 women writers

OLGA KENYON

LENNARD PUBLISHING
1989

Lennard Publishing
a division of Lennard Books Ltd
Musterlin House
Jordan Hill Road
Oxford OX2 8DP

British Library Cataloguing in Publication Data

Kenyon, Olga, 1932-
Women Writers Talk
1. Fiction in English. Women writers,
1900-1980 – Critical studies
I. Title
823'.912'099287

ISBN 1 85291 043 7

First published 1989
© Olga Kenyon 1989

Phototypeset in New Century Schoolbook
Design by Forest Publication Services, Luton
Cover design by Pocknell & Co.
Reproduced, printed and bound in Great Britain by
Butler & Tanner Ltd., Frome and London.

contents

women writers talk

introduction

Humour, politics, and experimentation energise women's writing today. Women are in the forefront of all major fictional forms, from the traditional story about relationships to the postmodernist novel. They are inventively, skilfully transforming a whole range - comedy, the saga, the poetic novella, the detective story, social satire. They have metamorphosed the gothic novel and science fiction.

This is a good time to assess women's achievements, two decades after the rebirth of the women's movement. It is in their writing even more than in society that women's vigour and potential is most remarkable. These ten women novelists have enlarged many forms of fiction. Fay Weldon, for example, has proceeded from writing television advertisements to major television productions; Nadine Gordimer has advanced from short stories to acute political analysis; Michele Roberts has moved from conventional forms to imaginative, metaphorical writing. Which areas concern women most at the moment? How will feminism develop in the near future? These writers offer their distinctive views in wide-ranging yet intimate interviews.

'Everything a writer has to say is in her work' maintain certain male critics, from Leavis in Cambridge to structuralists in France. But how did the novels come into being? Interviews provide valuable insights into the varied ways these different novelists approach the task of writing. Feminist critics stress the importance of women's experience, the particular social limitations and feelings of women in their writing. Interviews highlight female reactions to the process of writing, which cannot be gleaned from the finished product alone.

The mysterious process of creativity fascinates the

creative as well as the less creative reader. It is an aspect of human achievement which can rescue us from despair. It cannot be readily categorised. The interview, with its searching questions, reveals surprisingly different attitudes to creative drive. One novelist 'walks her characters up', to get to know them, like Henry James. Another rejects the very concept of character in favour of situation and feeling. Yet there are striking similarities. All stress the value of the subconscious and its mysterious workings, to which the artist must respond, while not fully comprehending its force.

Each writer has much to say of value on creative writing. Emma Tennant suggests breaking away from traditional forms, to see if the thriller or science fiction can release an unsuspected voice in oneself. Michele Roberts says that you must learn to love words for their own sake, not just use them as a means to an end. Fay Weldon recommends a practical adjunct, a felt-tipped pen to provide space for revisions.

Any aspiring writer who reads these interviews will find a diversity of experience to draw on, to help the imagination break out of its habitual channels. You can learn how to free yourself from writer's block by experimenting with the varied approaches of these novelists. All suggest fresh possibilities, because each is extending her chosen forms. They demonstrate the continuing strengths <u>and</u> versatility of the novel. It has become the most sensitive register of contemporary experience, while expanding the boundaries of expression and creativity.

The interview is a creative form in its own right. It provides a forum for writer and [sensitive] reader to explore areas neglected by critics. Indeed modern criticism which claims that subjective interpretation is as valid as the author's own, neglects the essential individual voice to which we respond when reading. Criticism would die if the writer ceased to respond to the personal creative urges which are the mainspring of writing, and the inspiration for this study.

This book explores how women write, why they write and how they read other women. Each interview is its own product, made of the relationship between two people responding to the interests, preoccupations, silences and warmth of the other. Creativity draws on memory, presents it in aesthetic form. The rhythms of speech duplicate the rhythms of the mind and provide us with further knowledge of the individual creator.

These interviews examine the origins and motivation for individual novels and a wider vision. They emphasise the distinctive way each writer responds with care, love, labour and invention to the primary tool of language. Use of autobiographical material is discussed, as are influences, the place and power of the subconscious, the artist's responsibility to others, to art, to self, to society.

My role has been to devise the questions beforehand and shape the interview afterwards. Some writers speak freely, others are more guarded, so the re-writing demands creativity - while respecting the thought of the author. Interviews provide first-hand accounts for appreciating a specific form of writing and learning more about the artist's notions and techniques. With these purposes in mind, I selected certain central areas to discuss: how they began; what helped (or hindered) their development; whether being female has made a great difference, or little, to their approach; what they think of writing today. Above all we discussed individual works, to discover their aesthetic intentions. It is vital to possess these alongside the interpretations of modern critics, to widen our conception of what the novel can achieve. For this reason I allowed the interviews to flow, to follow their ideas rather than impose a set pattern.

Why these ten Writers?
Each of the ten writers was selected as representing a distinctive approach to the novel, and developed a different genre.

Nadine Gordimer creates fiction out of the tensions experienced by individuals in a totalitarian regime.

Iris Murdoch exploits the strengths of the nineteenth century novel to analyse moral dilemmas through her characters.

P.D. James makes the detective story contemporary with her psychological insights, in a world where order is only partially restored.

Anita Brookner revitalises the romance as she fictionalises its restricting of female potential.

Fay Weldon constructs fresh forms, examining contemporary relationships and hang-ups in her acerbic, radicalising voice.

Emma Tennant is multi-faceted, exploring the potential of many genres to look at the psyche of adolescent girls and comment on comic weaknesses in England today.

Eva Figes is unusual in looking more to Europe than Britain. This has enriched the novel with sensitive exploration of states of mind.

Michele Roberts, a committed feminist, explores female experience through unusual metaphor. Her imaginative structures are extending the potential of fiction radically.

Alice Thomas Ellis writes brief comic fiction with many elements of the surreal, and with shrewd analysis of middle-class foibles and limitations. The gentle humour creates a new form of social satire like David Lodge's.

Margaret Drabble has been compared to George Eliot in her desire to comment on society, and contemporary issues. She has extended her range, through mothers' experience, to dilemmas of the late eighties.

They proved stimulatingly distinctive in interview. Iris Murdoch pondered her answers judiciously, Eva Figes would not judge trenchantly, Michele Roberts shared her enthusiasm for words, Margaret Drabble willingly answered any question while Fay Weldon humorously and unpretentiously talked about the topics which preoccupy her most.

Emma Tennant and P.D. James possess unusual fluency, answering in beautifully constructed sentences which need little revision. Others required encouragement, editing, second visits. Alice Thomas Ellis welcomed me into her warm kitchen, where we sat for two nights, exchanging ideas over drinks. Her warmth typifies the response of these women writers.

What they share is a warmth, an honesty, a responsiveness which can be called 'feminine'. Their qualities as people are markedly present in their writing. Their thoughtfulness and openness in responding to a wide range of questions justify the interview as a medium of literary criticism. Indeed their role as critics of their own work adds to our understanding of the complexities of the novel, throws new light on the role of gender in fiction writing. Interestingly the two most radical feminists resemble the two pre-feminists in their belief that male response is valuable, and a wish to explore male experience in fiction. The absence of polemic in an interview allows for a fruitful discussion of difference. I questioned all of them on the contemporary topic of how far they feel limited by patriarchal language, their range of response highlights the diversity displayed by women today.

All were generous in giving me their time, in

answering later questions and in revising my typescript.
When I met Iris Murdoch I had flu, so we agreed to use the
informative interview she gave David Gerard, which was
hitherto unpublished. Anita Brookner I met only briefly,
after she had won the Booker prize, but she kindly agreed
to my using her answers on that occasion and extracts
from her other interviews. When Nadine Gordimer came
to London after publishing A Sport of Nature she answered
some of my questions and generously agreed to my
including excerpts from her talk at the Institute of
Contemporary Arts in London and her interviews, made
by Thames Television, in the series Women Writers.

What these ten writers offer is a life-affirming
vision, at a time when most of us are less than it is in us
to be. They believe that it is possible to transform common
circumstance without injury. They help us to comprehend,
shape and re-envision our reality.

anita

brookner

ANITA BROOKNER was born in 1928

Novels
A Start in Life (1981)
Providence (1982)
Look at Me (1983)
Hotel du Lac (1984)
Family and Friends (1985)
A Misalliance (1986)
A Friend from England (1987)
Latecomers (1988)

Non Fiction
Watteau (1968)
The Genius of the Future (1971)
Greuze (1972)
Jacques-Louis David (1980)

K: Though you were born and educated in London, I have the impression that you have not wholly overcome the awareness that your parents were foreign?

B: I doubt that you ever get away from the people before you. My father was Polish-born, Jewish and alien. I have never learned the custom of the country, because we were Jews, tribal and alien. No one is free, although there are moments when you feel free, and these can be revelatory as well as exhilarating. I loved my parents painfully, but they were hopeless as guides. I am always trying to explain my family to myself and to others, to find out how I ended up in my peculiar situation. I do envy those who can take life a little more easily. I am too handicapped by expectations.

K: What sort of expectations?

B: The idea that right will triumph because this is England. It was implanted early by the novels of Dickens, which my father, who didn't understand the English, took to be true pictures of English life. He fed me with Dickens from the time I was seven, and I still re-read a Dickens novel every year. I am still looking for Nicholas Nickleby.

K: What were your mother's expectations?

B: She wanted me to be another kind of person altogether. I should have looked different, should have been more popular, socially more graceful, one of those small, coy, kittenish women who get their way. If my novels contain a certain amount of grief it is to do with my not being what I would wish to be. My mother was a singer who gave up her professional career when she married my father and was reduced to singing in our drawing room. She was inclined to melancholy and I believe she was very bored. She was very beautiful but lost her looks rapidly, and when she sang my father became restless and I would begin to cry: the nurse would take me away. It was the passion in the voice which showed, you see.

K: Did your parents ever talk about their past - or the holocaust?

B: No, and I'm grateful for that.

K: I believe you made plans to visit Poland, but didn't go. Why?

B: For a Jew, Poland is not exactly the Promised Land. I would have liked to see my father's family summer house on the river. But I would never have found it, or known if it was the right one and that would have mattered to me extremely.

K: Why did you choose to study in Paris after reading history in London?

B: I think you always feel braver in another language. And I realised that if I was a failure it was better to be a failure on my own terms. I lived very happily in Paris on £5 a week - for three years while writing my thesis on Greuze. I was liberated by poverty before I knew what the women's movement was all about.

K: Your books on art history are recognised worldwide. What is your view of your studies of David, Greuze and Watteau?

B: I think of them as steps in the painful process of self-realisation. I see myself as a speculative art historian rather than a scholar, and am sometimes worried that I might not be rigorous enough.

K: When you began teaching at the Courtauld did you enjoy it?

B: Rather to my surprise, I enjoyed teaching. I'm such a nervous person, I wouldn't have thought I'd be good at it. But the students were so <u>amiable</u>. They haven't yet learned those little hypocrisies. And if they trust you, then you must give them your <u>full attention</u>. That is why I could only write in the summer.

K: Anthony Blunt was at the Courtauld when you were there.

B: He's been very good to me: an excellent teacher. And he gave me my job. I valued him as a teacher and a friend.

K: Why is it that you didn't begin writing till middle age, like Edith Wharton? Had you been writing in secret?

B: No, there were no secret notebooks, not a scrap, not a sentence.

K: Why did you begin your first novel, <u>A Start in Life</u>?

B: Out of boredom and the wish to review my life, which seemed to be drifting in predictable channels. I saw it as a little exercise in self-analysis. What is interesting about self-analysis is that it leads nowhere. It is an art form in itself.

K: Do you rewrite a great deal?

B: No, there are no drafts, no fetishes, no false starts; there simply isn't <u>time</u>. I write straight onto a typewriter, as though the novels had been encoded in the unconscious. I find the process of writing painful rather than difficult. You never know what you will learn till you start writing. Then you discover truths you didn't know existed. These books are accidents of the unconscious. It's like dredging, really, seeing if you can keep it going.

K: Can you explain why you write when it's painful?

B: I can't really explain. I don't usually enjoy it. There's a terrible exhilaration, like having a high fever, which comes on me. Writing is my form of taking a sedative. It's almost a physiological process. When I'm actually writing, I feel so fantastically well. I even put on weight - and when it's all over, I feel ill.

K: Like Virginia Woolf.

B: There's not much choice between euphoria and illness.

K: Would you agree that your motivation sounds similar to that of some nineteenth-century women novelists?

B: Mine was a dreary Victorian story: I nursed my parents till they died. I write out of a sense of powerlessness and injustice, because I felt invisible and passive. Life is so badly plotted. The novel speaks about states of mind which forced me to do something about those states of mind.

K: So writing is a way of being your own analyst?

B: It would be extremely uncomfortable if it were. I think it gives a chance to examine certain things, within the limits of a structure, but with a certain amount of leisure. It's a meditative examination.

K: Was it difficult to get your first novel published?

B: It was turned down by three publishers before Liz Calder, at Jonathan Cape, spotted it, and decided to print.

K: What useful functions has writing had for you?

B: The function of writing for a marginal person is to reabsorb and redirect all the attention that has been wasted by too much listening and watching. This is a vital function for a passive person.

K: There are variations on that in your third novel <u>Look at Me</u>.

B: Yes. The heroine, Frances, tells us that writing is 'a penance for not being lucky'. It is an attempt to reach others and to make them love you.

K: That's your only novel in the first person. Do you like Frances?

B: I despised her for her susceptibility, her lack of divination, her stupidity. I felt myself getting madder and madder with her as I wrote it.

K: It was your fourth novel <u>Hotel du Lac</u> which brought you fame, with the Booker prize. Did that give you pleasure?

B: Enormous pleasure and enormous surprise.

K: One of the critics called it 'a Vermeer of a novel'. Vermeer has great stillness and depth. What image did you have in mind?

B: When I started the book, I simply wanted to write a love story in which something unexpected happened, and in which love really triumphed.

K: I thought you started with a hotel where you'd stayed in Switzerland?

B: I have stayed in that hotel more than once. Nothing like that happened in the real hotel, so I suppose that image did stay in my memory. It was very still; it was very grey; and one was waiting for something to happen.

K: Your heroine Edith is a novelist who looks like Virginia Woolf. Do you share any of Edith's characteristics?

B: Practically all of them, I should think. But I'm not going into detail.

K: What I mean is that it's a very personal story, isn't it?

B: Yes, I think it is. I meant it. Every word.

K: Do you find that being both a writer of novels and an academic art historian is a difficult balancing act to maintain?

B: It's a balancing act, but once you've got the hang of it, I think it's quite easy to continue. It's very difficult to stop either one or the other. You have to keep them both going.

K: Which do you regard as your central act, so to speak?

B: Somewhere in the middle, I think. Some people say I write fiction when I'm purporting to write fact, so maybe I'm in the middle all the time.

K: In your fiction you seem to me to give a very true picture of the way it is to be lonely, to be perceptive, to be an observer. Do you feel yourself to be those things?

B: I know all those things, intimately. Yes, I'm all those things.

K: You also show the contrast between the placid life of the Swiss hotel and her full life in London, which the heroine rejects for a time and then goes back to, because she cannot bear the greyness of life. Is that not the real balancing act, between those two poles?

B: Between isolation and gregariousness, yes. Between involvement and non-involvement. Yes, I think it is.

K: Would you say that one of the major themes is romantic love?

B: Romantic hopefulness - it's constant, in spite of a sense of defeat.

K: Isn't that a little old-fashioned today?

B: Romanticism is not just a mode; it literally eats into every life. Women will never get rid of just waiting for the right man.

K: You write about love, but little - overtly - on sexual matters.

B: These matters are private and should remain so. In fiction as in life. That's part of my old code, which I can't break.

K: You said to another interviewer that love is your subject.

B: What else is there? Everything else is merely literature. Real love is a pilgrimage. It happens when there is no strategy, but it is very rare because most people are strategists. So the chance of two non-strategists ever meeting is slight, and even if they do meet they may be deflected by the strategists.

K: Did you have to write slowly or did you kind it flowed easily?

B: I just wrote it once. I was lucky, it came out right.

K: Is it the novel of which you are most pleased?

B: No, I think the one I've just finished is better.

K: Your fifth novel is called <u>Family and Friends</u>. What made you want to write about a family?

B: It's my family. Of course they're rendered into fiction because I didn't know them till I was about seventeen - when I began to see them as separate people. They are made into fiction, but the memory of them is mine.

K: Wasn't it a family photograph which sparked this novel?

B: Yes, a cousin showed me a wedding photograph with my grandmother dominating the group, as she must have dominated the participants, whom I did not recognise. I gave the photograph back, but the following day I started to write <u>Family and Friends</u>. I had always avoided writing about my family. They had given me a good deal of trouble in real life.

K: So all the parents in your novels had been fictitious?

B: Yes, and to a certain extent, the early lives of these uncles and aunts are fictitious, for I knew nothing of their early lives and was obliged to invent them. But somewhere in the course of this invention, I discovered I was writing what amounted to a true chronicle. Whether this was an obscure form of unconscious memory, whether it was intuition, or whether it was the exhilaration of disposing of these characters whom I had always seen as immensely powerful, I have no idea.

K: So you felt freed by the writing?

B: Yes. I would get up every morning, go to my office and write without qualms until I felt it was time to go home. As I neared the end I was too frightened that

I might lose the conclusion - which I did not know yet - and so I merely sat in the garden and wrote in a notebook. I suddenly felt an enormous tension; but my ending, when it came, surprised me into laughter. I felt like a spectator at my own game.

K: Like Iris Murdoch, you feel there's an element of game-playing?

B: It was the game aspect of the whole enterprise which intrigued me; it had been set off by an accident, and it was a gamble whether it could be brought off. It enabled me to see those overbearing figures of immediate family as players in a game. That novel laid many ghosts for me. I hope I've given those ghosts something new to talk about. And I hope they are pleased with me.

K: Do you feel affection for Family and Friends?

B: It's the only one of my books I truly like.

K: You said that when writing Family and Friends you were in control. Is that a motive?

B: 'With one bound Jack was free.' It's that kind of involution almost. Maybe as in psychoanalysis you abreact the whole thing and it comes out right. The most amazing thing is that although I experienced these people in real life as terribly overpowering and basically unfair, I felt no anxiety in writing about them; I felt really affectionate. So maybe I unearthed something that was dormant. I'm very glad I did.

K: Do you ever write out of revenge?

B: No, not any more. I might have done once, but revenge doesn't go on for very long. You can't sustain it for more than one book. And I mean to be amusing rather than critical in <u>Family and Friends</u>.

K: You start that novel with a quote from Goethe stating that social rules may help, but can also hinder emotional development. Is that the premise on which the novel was based?

B: Absolutely. If you obey the rules, which you are taught to do, and the rules seem productive and praiseworthy, it's difficult to get away from them. But rules are to do with forms of control from which we must escape. So a conflict is set up quite early.

K: Is it a general conflict, or greater in this particular family?

B: I think it's more intense in this kind of European-Jewish family because of the desire, or rather <u>necessity</u> to keep together.

K: The novel is fairly schematic; four children, two of each sex, one of each gets away. Which was your mother?

B: My mother was Mimi, the good daughter, who stayed at home. She was extremely virtuous, and beautiful. My own mother was a singer, she did in fact have a career. She's a pattern for all daughters who stay at home, for whom I feel immense compassion.

K: What happened to her drive, her longing for freedom?

B: It got used up too early. However, I think repression has its uses - it sometimes leads to a fruitful late flowering when you realise you can break the rules at last. But if you break out too early and use all your freedom at once, then life does catch up with you, because nobody escapes. The two who break free early age badly. I remember noting that at the time - they become graceless. Whereas the ones who stayed at home and did their duty, and had been terribly unhappy doing it, had far more dignity. Maybe there's a kind of poetic justice about that. You wouldn't have thought the sacrifice was worthwhile, of course.

K: But the ones who got away thought they were entirely justified?

B: That's the way it goes.

K: Is the impulse to break free essentially immature?

B: Well, as a result of breaking the rules, they are entirely free. And free will is a heavy burden to lay on anyone, particularly if they are not too bright. They wonder what to do with it and why life hasn't gone on providing treats. And life doesn't.

K: Were they actually your aunt and uncle?

B: Yes, they were much in evidence. The two who had flown the nest, under somewhat disgraceful circumstances, used to pay lightning visits, loaded with presents, talking all the time, making good their escape before anyone recalled them to order. They left the good ones, who stayed at home, terribly discontented. It was sad, an object lesson in how to get your way - and how not to.

K: You've chosen a family saga, but concise, controlled, through a series of family photographs. Why did you choose that form?

B: Because it was easier. It was not a difficult book to write it was almost entirely free of anxiety. A chapter to each one is almost the easiest form. It was fascinating to write, as I could use the reaction of an art historian to the photographs.

K: Why did you decide to write about the <u>family</u> in <u>Family and Friends</u> instead of your usual solitary heroine?

B: The idea was precipitated into my mind by being shown that old family photograph. And I needed to get rid of the family. After all, the solitary heroine has a much longer life.

K: Are you tired of writing about solitary heroines?

B: Sometimes I'm fed up with them, but there's another on the horizon.

K: Your characters don't always seem in touch with the twentieth century.

B: Yes. These are nineteenth-century families, without the nineteenth century to give support.

K: That's their predicament?

B: Yes, they obey all nineteenth-century rules of morality and duty and seriousness, dedication and devotion without realising that these are important but anachronistic qualities. They come to this realisation too late.

K: So your family resembles your solitary heroine?

B: Yes, in that sense they are alike.

K: Your characters are not at home in the twentieth century. Is that why your heroines are given such a limited set of alternatives?

B: They are stupid - if they weren't they'd have more options. But the choice is never unlimited, that's the twentieth-century mistake, whereas the nineteenth century was more realistic. You can do this <u>or</u> that, not an unlimited number of things.

K: Is your writing a critique on the options of the twentieth century?

B: No, except that I find the moral position of many modern novelists ridiculous, as if you could start editing your life halfway through - and doing something for which you're unprepared. That's not feasible.

K: Did you write <u>Family and Friends</u> and <u>Latecomers</u> in order to have the chance to write about male characters?

B: I find them much more interesting, as I know about women.

K: Several of your women characters say they don't like women, they would rather be with men. Do you feel like that?

B: I love being with women, but I refer men's conversation. Mixed company is best, can't we agree on that?

K: I don't feel that today there's such a difference between the way men and women talk, though I feel it in Jane Austen.

B: Probably this is the first time since the Regency that men and women can converse on equal terms. But I grew up in an academy where I was taught by men and maybe I lean towards that sort of situation of being taught. I feel men's conversation is more instructive, or at least should be.

K: Yet women are at the centre of your novels, though you'd rather write about men?

B: I do like women, but it's stale to write about them all the time. I've just done it again. I now want to write about a hero. I want a hero, as Byron said.

K: Do you mind being described as a woman's novelist?

B: Not in the least. Women have devoted themselves to a certain kind of storytelling, which is extremely valid and extremely absorbing; mainly to other women, but to men as well, I think. It's a quite different genre. It does limit itself, but it tends to go deeper. Also it's full of information. Women tend to read novels for information - and to learn about other women, so the novel fulfils a particular function if it's written by a woman for other women.

K: Do you think you are read by men?

B: Yes, I do.

K: And read differently? How?

B: The most pertinent criticism I've had from a male reader is 'You write French books, don't you?' They don't offer comments on the characters, which women always do. Women tend to say 'You should have done so and so' or 'She would have done.' Men don't do this so much. They seem to view it from a certain distance. I haven't taken elaborate soundings, but I just know that the criticism tends to be different.

K: In all your novels there is tension between the self-sacrificing characters and those who grab. Why the opprobrium against those who grab at happiness?

B: I don't know why, because I think it's better to be a bad winner than a good loser. I don't think the meek inherit the earth. But I don't know the best way of getting what you want and feeling right about it - I wish I did.

K: You criticise those who get their own way. Does this offend some readers?

B: Yes, they write and criticise me. They feel I'm judging them, it's odd, and they feel they must get back at me. We all have terrible secrets, I'm sure, and it's not done to lift the lid on some of them.

K: Are the people who write the ones who have lost?

B: No, the people who have won. They write and say 'You don't know anything about it.'

K: And what do you write back?

B: I try to explain, but it's a lost cause.

K: You write like Edith Wharton, but with some of the preoccupations of Margaret Drabble. The heroine of your novel A Friend from England seems to find female independence a mixed emotional blessing.

B: Rachel has no close friends, she becomes a surrogate daughter to her accountant Oscar - and a friend to his own daughter, Heather. Female friendship is an undervalued and underfictionalised topic. I observe it through Rachel's measured introspection.

K: What else does the novel analyse?

B: It's almost the process of perception which goes on between the subjective person - 'I' - and friends; perceptions which we constantly have to revise. When you're in close contact with someone, you construct an image of them, then that image has to be revised and updated. This novel is about an unattached woman who finds herself confronted by a very secure family;

how she reacts to their behaviour.

K: Friendship is clearly an important topic here. Which qualities do you value most in a friend?

B: I think accountability, that's to say explaining actions with full knowledge of emotions and procedures. You get it in Russian novels: the complete confession. Accountability in friendship is the equivalent of love without strategy, and that is the <u>Grail</u>.

K: Finally, may I ask you what you think of novelists like Henry James?

B: He wars in my mind for supremacy with Dickens. If you wish <u>scrutiny</u>, then it has to be James - and the French. But if you want <u>indignation</u>, then it's Dickens.

K: And what about Proust?

B: Proust is very precious to me. That state of mind he kept himself in is so hypnotic and dangerous that one approaches rereading him almost with fear. Always marginal and always observing. The cost was too high when all is said and done. The perils of remaining in that childlike state of receptivity are terrifying. And the awful thing is that he got it right <u>all the time</u>. It is all true.

margaret

drabble

MARGARET DRABBLE was born in
Sheffield in June 1939

Novels   A Summer Bird-Cage (1963)
      The Garrick Year (1965)
      The Millstone (1965)
      Jerusalem the Golden (1967)
      The Waterfall (1969)
      The Needle's Eye (1972)
      The Realms of Gold (1975)
      The Ice Age (1977)
      The Middle Ground (1980)
      The Radiant Way (1987)

Plays   Laura (for Television, 1964)
      Bird of Paradise (1969)

Screenplays Isadora (with Melvyn Bragg &
       Clive Exton, 1969)
      A Touch of Love (1969)

Non Fiction Wordsworth (1966)
      Virginia Woolf: A Personal Debt (1973)
      Arnold Bennett: A Biography (1974)
      A Writer's Britain: Landscape in
       Literature (1979)
      The Oxford Companion to English
       Literature (as editor, 1985)

Juvenile   For Queen and Country: Britain in the
       Victorian Age (1978)

K: What do you think of women's writing at the moment?

D: This is a subject on which I've thought and written for the last twenty years. In 1968 I taught a course on Women's Writing. I believe it was one of the first, though I soon realised many others were beginning. It was a subject which was bubbling up and became formalised as Women's Studies. I planned a course of English writers from Austen to Lessing. And we included almost the first book of feminist criticism, by Mary Ellmann, who looks at the way women have been treated through history. It's all familiar now but was very new then. She took on subjects still being discussed, such as why women writers are thought of in a more familiar way than men - we say Edith Wharton, instead of using the surname. We were groping towards analysis of what made women different.

K: And what was your own view?

D: My own view was, and still is, that there was a whole generation of young women writers like myself who had been brought up to believe that the world was open to their talents. That they were free to go to college, pursue a career, have a job, marriage and children. This was something that women in the nineteenth century had hardly ever achieved with the glorious and honourable exception of Georges Sand. In Britain, only Mrs Gaskell combined the two. Charlotte Bronte was much more archetypal and her rage and frustration, as she admitted, flowed into her books.

When we left college we had babies, fed the family, did a day's work, served Cordon Bleu meals by candlelight and were free to have intellectual conversation all evening. But the freedom was a mockery because we were all overloaded, exhausted. And out of that feeling arose the women's novel of the sixties, it just arose spontaneously: Edna O'Brien, Doris Lessing, Penelope Mortimer, and a little later Fay Weldon, beginning to express these feelings of rage. We were not actually blaming men but we felt caught in a trap and did not know how to get out. I think there is a real generation gap between writers like Iris Murdoch who is slightly older and does not have children and rather dismisses the feminist case because she does not admit it exists.

K: What were the important new elements in women's novels of the sixties?

D: Domestic squalor and domestic strife and the conflict between career and children. It built on the traditions of the nineteenth century, and took a new shape. By the seventies it grew increasingly angry and controversial.

K: How do you see feminist writing changing then?

D: It became more separatist and split off. The dates are interesting. It's one of the only historical movements that I've lived through, of which I feel I've marked every pointer. I remember in 1968 Angus Wilson gave an address on 'Changing Sexual Attitudes'. He said that if men didn't change their attitudes, women would demand Amazonian warfare. When I say new subject matter and attitudes grew then, I do not want to exclude some men. I consider Angus Wilson's novel <u>The Middle Age of Mrs Elliott</u> one of the best novels from a woman's point of view by a man. There were some men who positively took part in the move towards a different kind of respect for the woman's domestic life and interior life.

K: Which further developments helped women, in your view?

D: Various technical developments especially the Virago Press, founded in 1977 and The Women's Press in 1978. They not only risked money by publishing new work of quality, but also rediscovered the tradition of forgotten writers. They have reprinted many important women such as Rosamund Lehmann and Mary Webb, perhaps not classics, but part of a major tradition, which filled in a lot of the gaps.

K: What other changes do you see as important?

D: When interviewed to revise the Oxford Companion to English Literature in 1979 I said I would include entries on Feminist Criticism and Feminist Publishing. I was told: 'Don't worry dear, it will take you five years and then it will all have gone away.' But now men realise it's all here to stay. However, a problem with a movement that receives critical attention is that it becomes the focus of its own self destruct. Women begin to complain that they are being put on Women's shelves in libraries, that they are in a ghetto. Some have felt themselves trapped by their own reputation as women writers, such as Doris Lessing. She achieved fame, indeed notoriety for <u>The Golden Notebook</u> in 1962. She became spokesperson for the American Women's movement, without her consent.

K: Surely she broke away with her science fiction and Jane Somers books?

D: Her opening of the second Jane Somers is playing a game with Mills and Boon romances. Like Anita Brookner's Edith Hope, but more devious. Both are anti-romantic and romantic at the same time. Women have not thrown away the notion of the romantic novelist, romance, the dark stranger, love.

K: Do you consider we can validly differentiate between the ways men and women write?

D: I think there is a difference between male and female prose. I have come to no conclusions, but I would maintain that there are many instances where one can tell, from a paragraph, if not from a sentence. Unless the narrator is deliberately using pastiche, or a different persona, as Iris Murdoch notoriously and brilliantly does, writing as a male psyche. Though the Brontes wrote under deliberately androgynous pseudonyms, they were rumbled quite quickly. Charlotte sooner than Emily, as it's scarcely conceivable that <u>Jane Eyre</u> could have been written by a man. Jane Austen has all the quiet confidence of a female writer who doesn't listen to anybody telling her what to do. Doris Lessing in <u>The Golden Notebook</u> could only be female, Dorothy Richardson in <u>Pilgrimage</u> could only be a woman. Virginia Woolf, though she wrote about androgyny, has a woman's sensibility, approach and subject-matter. Of course she devoted the whole of <u>A Room of One's Own</u> to discussing whether the writing of a woman is different. It's she who maintained that Dorothy Richardson's prose is 'feminine', because of her unpunctuated sentences. I have heard it asserted that punctuation is essentially male, a segmenting, with brutal commas and full stops dividing what ought to be the free associative flow of the mind. But remember that some of the greatest free associative prose was written by that aggressively male character James Joyce. It's true that he put much of his female prose into the mind of Molly Bloom. Nevertheless it shows that men also think in an unpunctuated, associative, freely flowing way.

K: Is there a long tradition of self-consciousness about whether one is male or female as a writer?

D: Yes, it came to a crisis in the seventies, associated with the feeling that we were living a new life, with new pressures and new possibilities.

K: What did you find when lecturing on this in Germany?

D: They don't have nineteenth-century women novelists of the kind we are supported by, the strength of tradition that we have built on. I was interested, talking to students in Hamburg, that the word feminist has a much more hostile connotation there; in Britain people mean they support equal pay, etc. In Germany it means you are an active campaigner and a provocative speaker. If one doesn't know the reverberation of a word in another country one can't know what one is implying when saying, as I usually do, 'Yes I'm a feminist but.'

K: And in America?

D: It's got a higher profile, because their movement was more associated with Betty Friedan and Kate Millett. It was more political, about entering the workplace, where they have been more successful than we have. Some of their writing is aggressive, more outspoken than ours. Some of their mainstream writers such as Erica Jong, Liza Alther are also writing in a manner that many English feminists would consider risqué, or over the top.

K: You have lectured in Japan, haven't you?

D: Yes, and been sent books which they are publishing now. I stayed in Japan with a divorcee of about my age who wrote beautiful English and studied my contemporaries. Yet the more I talked to her the more I realised our lives are utterly dissimilar. She was waited on by her mother, had an old aunt locked up in a small room, whom I was not allowed to meet. The whole social set-up was to me impenetrable. You think you have made a contact, when whole realms of difference open up. The novel is the easiest way of penetrating another culture, of striking up some kind of friendship. My Japanese hostess and I knew each other better through our books than we could ever know each other in real life.

K: What did you find in India?

D: There's quite a lot of feminism, in different forms. The most outspoken novelist is Camilla Das, writing about women's bodily problems. In that same country you can have an incredibly emancipated conversation in Delhi or Madras; while in a small university, you find the sexes sitting in separate groups. In one, the girl students all told me they'll get married after their degrees, yet a young man came to say he was researching on phallic imagery in Erica Jong, Margaret Atwood and Liza Alther.

K: And what's the situation in New Zealand, with writers like Keri Hulme?

D: New Zealand is one step ahead of us. Women writers are using an exciting mix of Anglo-Saxon and Maori traditions. They are experimental and interesting. The younger ones seem to be living in a very different society from their parents - Patricia Grace, Sue Mcauley, Keri Hulme. I caused mortal offence by not mentioning Katherine Mansfield enough; she's very much a pioneer as she wrote in a liberated manner long before it was considered acceptable.

Her lifestyle was liberated, and as Claire Tomalin's recent biography has suggested, it caused her death, from venereal disease. The Booker prize winners of the 1970s were all riddled with various forms of sexual disease. It formed part of the liberation of women, that we began to complain of things that had been unmentionable in the 1950s. Suddenly there was this outburst of gynacological and obstetric complaints. Now we have the more tragic problem of

AIDS which is producing its own literature. Before the AIDS terror hit us, women aired a lot of their obstetric problems for the first time. Of course men don't find that particularly interesting, but it was a phase that had to be gone through.

K: Now you've gone through that phase and reached The Radiant Way?

D: Well, I started and stopped it various times. I wanted this novel to cover a period of time, to be seen through the eyes of three principal women characters; and I knew I wanted to end it on a pastoral note - though I couldn't work out how to do it. I knew the subject-matter but not the incident or the plot. Sticking a northern part and a London part together was extremely difficult technically. I had a vision of what it had to be, but did not know how to do it. I wanted the murderer to be there, but wasn't quite sure how much murder to have in the book, or whether to let it come so close to them. It's a Dickensian motif, but in Dickens he would have murdered one of the principal characters, whereas in mine he murdered one of the marginal ones.

K: But you knew the end before you began writing?

D: Yes, but the end is only a mood isn't it? I knew the women would have a sort of epilogue with mixed feelings about their future and the past. The material had been brewing for five or six years as I hadn't written a novel during that time.

K: The Standard hailed this novel as 'important', were you pleased?

D: I'd like to think The Radiant Way is an important book. It's not prophetic. I'm recording, and I think that can be useful. An important role for a writer is simply to use your eyes and tell the truth, I also think there is a moral basis to my work - though I feel more tentative about saying this. Some people hate the use of the word 'moral' as it sounds pious. But I do write from a sense of the worth of all human beings which I hope comes through in the books. It certainly comes through in the writers I admire most. It's there in Lessing - and Zola who wrote about the whole of French society. They are tackling large subjects and I admire that. I'd like to think I write books which might contribute to a way of seeing British society.

K: You've been compared to Dickens. Does that please you?

D: It fills me with fear because he's such a great writer. But I do find Dickens inspiring. At the moment I'm turned on by Dickensian coincidence and the way his narrative, which appears to be naturalistic, is extremely unreal. In the novel I'm just finishing, I use a lot of that. He uses social observation and creates scenes to say something peculiar of his own. I'm flattered though slightly overawed by the comparison.

K: Do you feel criticised for not living up to a label imposed by others?

D: Absolutely. I don't think I really am a Dickensian writer. The label got stuck because I'm interested in sociology and so was Dickens; and my novels are getting longer. I'm expected to do a Dickensian survey of London life. If only I could live up to it, I'd be happy.

K: Like many nineteenth-century novelists, you like to address the reader?

D: It's now called post-modernism, but the Victorians called it the narrator speaking directly to the reader. A lot of novelists do it today; John Fowles, Malcolm

34

Bradbury, David Lodge. What we are doing is assuming that the reader is as intelligent as we are, knows what we are doing and is able to dissent. There's a sort of dialogue going on. The omniscient narrator is disappearing. Yet many people prefer the idea that the novel sprang from nowhere and is completely self-contained, so that you can suspend your disbelief, and believe it's a true story. Even Tolstoy, quoted as the great realist, was always lecturing you, great pages about his theories on history, about Napoleon, about politics.

K: You are interested in politics too. Yet The Radiant Way appears pessimistic from a political standpoint.

D: Yes, it was meant to be. I am depressed; we ought to have got a bit further by now. I see a terrible failure of nerve in the political and educational system. They are going to sell the National Health Service. Even the underpinning is being taken away after all our progressive dreams. I think our society is mad, and we will look back on these dark days with disbelief. Public spending is now wasted money. To clean streets gives pleasure and useful employment. There's nothing more useful than the middle class making a fuss. I'm absolutely against paying your way out.

But what I wanted to show in The Radiant Way is that even when you're living in a hostile climate politically, you yourself can live well, have a good life, supper with your friends. I was trying to contrast a constrained public life with a rich personal life. And I do think that's possible, on every social level, not just for the middle-class. I wanted to show that Brian's working-class father in the North had a perfectly good life although he was a widower; he had a nice flat, pot plants, friends; he was concerned, he was on the committee for the housing estate. It's a question of what you are when things are against you that's most important.

K: And what happens in volume two?

D: My publisher may consider it's completely mad. They go up north and Alex finds that her left-wing husband Brian is quite normal up there; he is no longer pushed into an extreme position by agitators. It's a question of finding the right environment for yourself - if you're considered a nutter in the environment you're in. I wanted to say that Brian is not really mad.

K: There must be something satisfying about writing a sequel?

D: Yes, you give yourself a second chance. But people you thought you had wrapped up and put away say 'You can't get rid of me so easily.'

K: Why don't younger people get a look in?

D: That's not my subject. The three women are central - slightly older than my age group, so slightly more trapped. You also have to look at them in psychological terms; they are the children of these women. So Liz Headland's children have special problems. The son of Alex's first marriage is very nice and successful - I saw some of his paintings yesterday in a Bond Street gallery.

K: Did you mean these women to seem successful or not?

D: Neither, though I'm extremely interested in readers' reactions to this. Liz is the career woman who makes good money and lives in a big house. There is a slight indication that she is a little unscrupulous. In career terms she can be considered successful, though the husband leaves her. The other two are much more comprehensible to me. They are people who have muddled along, after a very good education. They teach part-time and never get themselves on the career ladder - typical of that generation. But I did suggest in Polly a dynamic woman who is going to do extremely well in the man's world. I was annoyed with an American critic who complained that these women were too successful; they obviously have not done anything like as much as they could do with their lives. Liz has more personal problems, turning her back on her family.

K: Would you say your books deal with women more than men?

D: No I wouldn't. The early ones certainly did, because when I started, I was writing out of a narrow domestic situation. The Radiant Way is not a women's book, it's about the decline of western civilisation. It's seen through women's eyes, but it's not mainly about women.

K: Tell me something about the male characters, especially Wolpe.

D: He's a Satanist anthropologist. This was my little joke about magic realism, a sort of response to it. I'm interested in the way the irrational fits into the rational world. We all call ourselves rationalists, and live in a secular world, yet most of us glance at horoscopes occasionally, though we've got rid of a lot of superstitious nonsense since the Enlightenment. Claudio Wolpe is meant to be a rationalisation of the irrational, of weird obsessions. There are some real Italian scholars, of whom the most famous is Mario Praz, who wrote The Romantic Agony, who would call down the wrath of heaven on their enemies. I wanted a symbol of the extraordinary contrasts in our intellectual life today.

K: Were you also suggesting that characters like that are destructive?

D: Nothing so all-embracing, but the occult can be bad for you. People are often attracted towards things that can undo or destroy them.

K: Do you start with an idea or a personality - or something else?

D: Usually an idea. In The Radiant Way it was what went wrong in the 1980s. Then you think of characters and situations and plots to embody it. In The Mill Stone I wanted to write about how far motherhood changed people's characters. The character arose out of this fairly abstract question.

K: Do you find some characters becoming an embarrassment?

D: Occasionally, though I don't kill them off as much as some authors do. When the book remains schematic it's boring. When characters become inconsistent you know they are real. In The Radiant Way if you just had Liz being Truth, Esther interested in Beauty and Alex in the Good, or Marxism, Freud and Aesthetics, that would be boring. It's when they start overlapping and quarrelling that you know they're real. Once characters get their own dynamics, they start speaking for themselves.

K: How much do you have to cut?

D: In the new novel I've just finished I had to take out one whole story line. You do put in things that aren't going to work. I never redraft the whole, but some parts are rewritten endlessly.

K: How much do your editors edit?

D: It varies. They make suggestions, which I don't usually listen to if I consider they deal with integral parts of the book. But it's terribly useful to have an editor point out anachronisms. For example there was a character in The Radiant Way who listens to cassettes in her car - that was just not possible then. A good editor is invaluable, so is a good translator.

K: You are being translated widely - do the translations please you?

D: It's a fascinating topic - what one culture reads into another. I've had a correspondence over two translations of The Radiant Way, one into French, the other into Danish. The questions from my French translator are superb, wonderfully interesting and amusing. One is about the starfish and the stella marina. He says 'Why call them different names when these are the same thing in French? I think I'm going to call them 'asterix radieuse'.' I replied you've got the right idea. He asked about Camden Lock, whereas the other translator asked about the base lending rate, pay differentials, almost an economic quiz. All the translators have got lost on satellites and dish receivers. I had put in the jargon without knowing exactly what it means.

K: So you need not understand every area? Do you think that's why magic realism has gained so many readers in the last decade?

D: That's an interesting theme - I have a theory that magic realism by women is different from men's. In this country there are quite a lot of women writing about witches. It's magic but not exactly like Marquez, it's more Nordic, in the Tales of Hoffmann tradition. I gave a lecture in Spain last year on witchcraft as so many are writing about it; Fay Weldon in Puffball, Angela Carter in The Magic Toyshop.

K: It's entirely different from what you do, how much do you like it?

D: I find it attractive, though it's not something I want to do. But for women magic is helpful; as is the rewriting of fairytales. Sara Maitland has written a lot of upside-down fairy stories. You take a known story and plot and show how history has always told it one way and you tell it another way. It's using magic legitimately - but quite differently from Salmon Rushdie's use of it. There's a Scandinavian writer called Maria Tikkenen telling Red Riding Hood as an obvious sex story.

K: Who were strong influences on you? I know you admire nineteenth-century novelists and said you prefer to be at the end of that dying tradition.

D: Well, many writers have influenced me, especially Wordsworth. He means several things to me. One is the dawn of Romanticism, which was full of high political aspirations, a belief in every man, that we are all equal, that we shall all move forward together - everything that was good in the French Revolution. Of course he turned conservative later, but when he was young his hope was contagious. He wrote wonderfully about the good that is in everyone. Wordsworth made it clear that a little is enough, if we all lived in a community, and shared more. I have just written an article about this, that it would be better for us all to receive the same, which would be much less for some. I got letters saying it would be impossible. To this day I find him moving on the dignity of rather dull work, the dignity of motherhood. Also he writes about the natural world in such a way that one feels one can be restored for one's failure in human relationships. If I'm feeling really depressed I go for a walk alone in the country, my heart lifts up and I feel restored, a better person; it's a simple relevation, but

Wordsworth seems to be the first to have had it. How did they manage so long without it? I went for a walk in Kew Gardens yesterday, it was a beautiful day and I agree with Wordsworth that you will do yourself more good by going for a walk than doing many other things.

K: May I ask a rather superficial question? What makes you prefer to put things on paper rather than tell us orally - by lecturing?

D: I don't think that's a superficial question. It's so profound I can't answer it. I enjoy talking and the opportunity it gives of going to other places and seeing what's going on there and that becomes material for the next book. There's something about writing, not a demon, nothing as dramatic as that, rather a feeling that's the way I can seriously express myself. When I talk I say a lot of superficial things and wish I hadn't. Whereas when I'm writing I've got time to make patterns, to think.

K: How is storytelling linked to that?

D: I always say I'm not interested in storytelling, but I am interested in stories as vehicles for ideas. And I'm certainly interested in character and personality. I wouldn't want to write something that's all plot. There's a woman writer who does both: Ruth Rendall. She constructs magnificent plots under her Barbara Vine name, A Fatal Inversion and A Dark Adapted Eye. Her psychological thrillers make me weep with envy - they are so beautifully, superbly plotted. Yet there is sufficient psychological fascination for one to be completely gripped by the characters. That's a rare combination which looks effortless, but I can't do it.

K: How far do you feel an artistic difficulty in communicating with your audience?

41

D: I suspect my audience is fairly narrow. They write to me, they are the sort of people who would be my friends and picking up my children if I lived in Kidderminster. I sometimes put in a joke or insult especially for them. But there are a lot of other people who read me, like the Japanese, and what is it they are reading? Yes there is an uncertainty. You could say there is an inner circle whom I know quite well, but beyond that there are bigger and bigger circles about whom I know nothing at all. At times you meet people who would never normally read you. Last year I gave some talks in prisons, it was fascinating, because you get reactions from men who would never usually read novels.

That experience makes you realise there's no such thing as a 'universal' book, but merely books, which only reach a certain range of people.

K: Have you tried writing for the theatre?

D: I considered playwriting, but I wasn't very good. The world of the theatre is much more difficult for women than for men; that's one of the generalisations that's actually true. Writing novels is easier, publishers take women's novels seriously, whereas women can have a rough time in the theatre. I wrote a one-act play for the National Theatre in an evening of women's plays, but it wasn't a terribly interesting experience for me, I never quite knew what I was doing. I wrote one play for television which was alright, but not more. I didn't enjoy the process of messing around and trying to get it to the right length. I'm a very private worker.

K: Have you ever written any poetry?

D: I used to write some at school, I'd like to because I quite often have thoughts that would fit better into poetry - but I can't write poetry. I was in Hamburg recently with Maureen Duffy. She's a very interesting writer, who began as a playwright, but she just encountered too many obstacles, and took to the novel. Now she's also a marvellous poet. In Hamburg she read a wonderful poem about her mother, who is a dressmaker, with an image of shears of fate. You could hear every snip of the shears as the mother cut out her material on a hard table. What a wonderful gift to be able to write a page of poetry instead of having to put that whole character into a novel and build structures round it - but I can't do it. She's multiply gifted. It's interesting to speculate that she might have been a great playwright; but there comes a time when one doesn't want to go on battling. (I feel too much awe to attempt poetry.)

K: But surely novel-writing is terribly hard work?

D: Yes. A novel is quite an investment of time. You've got to have staying power which a lot of people don't have. It takes character to keep on at the point when you feel like throwing it away. Philip Larkin said he preferred poems because if you write a bad poem you've only wasted a week, whereas if you write a bad novel you waste a whole year.

K: And what do you prefer writing with? Fay Weldon recommends felt-tip pens.

D: I have an old manual and use two fingers. At least you can control it, whereas the electric typewriter goes too fast.

K: What about a word-processor? Russell Hoban loves his.

D: Word-processors are wonderful for bad typists or for articles. When I tried using it for writing fiction, the result was so bad and diffuse, I threw it away.

K: Do you enjoy readers writing to you with their opinions?

D: I enjoy it very much; any writer feels the day is brighter when they get a nice letter in the post. I have a great deal of correspondence but by no means all friendly.

K: Angela Carter receives suggestions about how to change her characters.

D: I get letters about why did you make her stay with that terrible man, you haven't been fair.

K: How English. I suppose far more women write to you than men?

D: Well far more women read novels than men. Perhaps women have a little more time than men during the day?

K: Do men tend to read lighter fiction, detective stories?

D: Sometimes men say 'Which of your novels should I read, my wife says they are quite good?' I feel aggrieved, as they are putting me into the Mills and Boon category. Whereas what they really mean is that they are not up to reading a demanding novel. According to a recent survey, men read more thrillers, history and biography.

K: Do you enjoy writing biography?

D: No, it's too like hard work. It is a demanding specialised task. When I wrote on Arnold Bennett I was not free to go to New York to look at the original documents. And with three small children I hadn't the money.

K: But you went to the Black Country and wrote some impressive descriptions of his birthplace.

D: I haven't got the stamina or perhaps the commitment for the fifteen years' dedication needed for something like the biography of G.B.Shaw [Which her second husband Michael Holroyd is writing.]

K: May I ask you about previous novels? What led you to start writing?

D: The startled astonishment that it was difficult to be free and a mother. My first three novels were written during my three pregnancies. Being a writer was a good compromise, you could stay at home and be professional. There were undercurrents of rage, though they are veiled conpared to later writing. My protests were mild, but I felt I had to express them. This was the first time women novelists dealt frankly with subjects not considered 'polite', such as breastfeeding, hysterectomy, wanting too much. Later in the sixties our expectations were lowered, the wit grew sourer. Men traditionally can have both a domestic life and outside work; our greed for both had been awakened and was not being satisfied.

K: But did you realise all this in your first, <u>A Summer Birdcage</u>?

D: When I started I was not conscious of myself as a woman writer. Then I realised there were parallels with Victorian novelists: I was bored, lonely, needed money. I had no sense of conscious feminism. I began modestly with no encouragement, or discouragement, from anybody. In a tradition which includes Jane Austen and George Eliot there is no need to feel apologetic. But some women must feel a sense of hesitation since I am so often asked if I did. The answer in my case is that a conventional university education gave me confidence in my opinions. I had been taught to think for myself, not parrot others, both at school and university. But I wasn't sure what my subject-matter was in those early novels. It was domestic, inevitably connected with babies, as I found them fascinating. I thought I had a whole new world that other people hadn't written much about. That encouraged me to carry on, so did the letters I received, and reading Doris Lessing. Also there was nothing else I could get to grips with outside, I was a sort of prisoner. As the children grew older, I saw one could write a different sort of novel, do research, travel. I'm deeply ashamed that I could not travel while writing on Arnold Bennett. But the restraint is connected with the great joy of bringing them up.

K: And when they grew up and went to nursery school?

D: Miracle of miracles. I could get out for walks, look round London, That's expressed in <u>A Needle's Eye</u>. I attended law courts, enjoyed the forays outside, meeting other people to get information, do research

K: How much do you plan before writing?

D: I have a plan in my head, but I never write it down and I often diverge from it. Some writers put down a chapter by chapter analysis, but for me a novel is a kind of exploration of an unknown goal, so I allow myself to change direction quite frequently. There is usually a point about halfway through when I can see the rest of the plan. That's a really satisfying moment for me. I suspect one of the advantages of my method is the feeling of exhilaration towards the end. Those who plan in detail can become bored halfway through, because they know where everything is going.

K: When do you titles come to you?

D: That varies very much; most of them come in the middle. But I could not think of a title for <u>Middle Ground</u>. In the end it was my publishers who thought of the title. This betrays something - that I couldn't think of the main theme, decide what it was centrally about. Whereas with <u>The Ice Age</u> I had no difficulty; it seemed to play off <u>The Realms of Gold</u>; one icy cold book against a warm one in the Sahara.

K: Do you discuss the novel while you're writing?

D: No, I'm too protective at that stage, I often feel it's too silly for others to look at it. I will talk about technical aspects, see geologists, discuss what their life is like, see how much I can use. But I wouldn't discuss the actual writing of the book because I don't know fully what I'm doing myself and I feel it's too raw to be exposed at that stage.

K: Do you keep reading back what you've already written?

D: I'm not sure; I suppose I do. Sometimes there are small inconsistencies one has to check on. If the plot is fairly complicated, like the two recent ones, I have to make sure the characters are in the right place.

K: Where does the title <u>Realms of Gold</u> come from?

D: Well, it's Keats 'Much have I travelled in the realms of gold', from the sonnet 'On first looking into Chapman's Homer'. I wanted to suggest that the protagonist Frances has literally travelled to the realms of gold, because she goes off into the Sahara where she finds gold bars. She's very lucky as an archaeologist as most people only find bits of pots, whereas she finds little gold bars. It's a symbol of luck, it's also a symbol of the imaginative process. Somewhat portentous, but luck is digging in the right place and the creative bit is guessing where the right place is.

The combination of chance and choice in writing a novel is fascinating. I wanted to indicate that these worlds of the imagination exist and can be entered and that one has a freedom to create oneself a good future. It's an optimistic title and meant to be. It was translated into French as <u>L'Age d'Or d'une Femme</u> - typically French. I went to see my publishers in Paris who gave me a wonderful lunch, scarcely spoke to me till the end when they told me what sort of man Frances should have had an affair with. That is not the translation I would have chosen as it confines it to her enjoying her middle age, which was not meant entirely, because it deals with imaginative creation.

K: Do they not allow you any say in the translation of titles?

D: No, and it's usually too late. When I commented on this, they replied 'Oh she's been so ill, we can't tell her.' It's a strange feeling to think that the books have gone into another realm, where you have no control.

K: Do they consult you on jackets?

D: Sometimes, but I never object. I trust my publishers to have more expertise than me, as I'm not very good on typography.

K: Do you find yourself identifying with some of your characters?

D: That's a tricky problem. I write with more personal detail about some bits, then you begin to identify yourself, then readers identify you. I was slightly abrupt in <u>The Realms of Gold</u> in saying 'She's not me.'

K: But don't you think you have to begin with yourself?

D: For me that was essential, but with growing confidence

and experience, one can then move further away. However, there are no rules. There is the notorious example of Susan Hill. Her first novels were about old ladies in Cheltenham. Then she wrote about young men in the First World War. She's unusual in that she chooses to write at one remove, with inevitably distant subject matter.

K: What advice have you got for aspiring writers?

D: Decide what sort of book you've written, choose the publisher of books most like yours, send a chapter and a covering letter. There's no point sending a romance to a publisher of thrillers. Here's some good advice: as there are lots of prizes, it's well worth looking at the leaflet called <u>Literary Prizes</u> to see what's there. I've just been judging one, for people under thirty-five, and they read unpublished as well as published novels. The Book Trust is very helpful as it's their job to disseminate information about publishers, their address is East Hill, Wandsworth. Good luck.

alice

thomas

ellis

ALICE THOMAS ELLIS was born in Liverpool before
the Second World War.

Novels	The Sin Eater (1977) The Birds of the Air (1980) The 27th Kingdom (1982) The Other Side of the Fire (1983) Unexplained Laughter (1985) The Clothes in the Wardrobe (1987) The Skeleton in the Cupboard (1988)
Non Fiction	Natural Baby Food (as Anna Haycraft, 1978) Darling, You Shouldn't Have Gone to So Much Trouble (as Anna Haycraft, with Caroline Blackwood, 1980)
Collected Journalism from *The Spectator*	Home Life (1986) More Home Life (1987) Home Life Three (1988)

K: Can you tell me what made you start to write?

E: Frustration. Everyone seemed to be talking about poor little me at the kitchen sink. Some people seemed to think women had no power at all. Whereas in my family all the women were strong and powerful personalities.

K: This second phase of feminism is rediscovering that, don't you think?

E: Yes, that's true. In the sixties I was an art student so I'd gone through all the longing for a freer life style and free love - then suddenly everyone discovered it.

K: And did you paint after you finished studying art?

E: Only my children. That portrait over the mantelpiece is one of them.

K: I like it, it catches a turn-of-the-century style. I can see now why there's such telling visual detail in some of your novels. Do you have to work hard at writing, since you began creating as a painter?

E: No, I never feel I have to rewrite or redraft.

K: And how much time do you spend planning before you write?

E: Very little. Once you've made up your characters, you can let them loose - as one does a little bit with one's family.

K: But sometimes you set yourself a difficult task, don't you?

E: Yes, with <u>Twenty-Seventh Kingdom</u> I decided to invent a woman who is very good and very beautiful, and convinces people she was true; and happens to be black.

K: What other ideas spark off your novels?

E: Different ideas of romantic love in <u>The Other Side of the Fire</u>. I like to do something almost impossible - there it was to make credible the woman in love with her stepson, the younger man. I don't believe in romantic love, so I compare various women's attitudes to love and the soap opera which that appalling girl is writing. What are they talking about when they talk about romance? Where is the evidence? I suppose there are a few happy marriages which one can count on one hand, and they're bored with each other. But I'm asking 'How on earth has it got to such a pitch that people seem to think it makes the world go round?'

K: It's interesting to compare you with Anita Brookner, coming to the novel at roughly the same age, writing harrowingly about romantic love.

E: Yes I read that she wanted six children, that's nuts. I suppose an advantage of being married is that one doesn't have to go to the grave still longing to find a husband.

K: What do you think of feminism today?

E: I think it's getting more reasonable, don't you? In the thirties we were getting to a proper view and now we are having to do it again. Of course so many things happen in history, there's not just one thread. It's exhausting, always having to start again. And men just don't understand women. Take this article in the <u>Financial Times</u> today by Lawrence Durrell repeating that women are only good for one thing. Once women stop being loyal to Henry or Horace or Cecil, and talk to other women, they will lose a whole heap of neuroses and anxieties and insecurities. Go to the garden fence and talk <u>honestly</u> to the lady next door; it's better than valium.

K: Wouldn't that help men too?

E: Men don't like to see themselves as imperfect or flawed, whereas women don't mind looking for help or support; so many men can't.

K: What do you think of your male characters?

E: I think of men the way Durrell thinks of women, as mostly, though not invariably, dreadfully dull. For an evening out, I'd rather go with a bunch of women any day. If you want to laugh, get together with some women. Some of my aunts were really humorous; my Aunt Marion was the funniest person I've ever met. And my friends at school were terribly funny too. We refused to work hard at our grammar school. In fact I was expelled.

K: What did you do then?

E: They allowed me back to take the Higher Certificate in Art, then I went on to study at Liverpool College of Art. I had no idea at the time that I might become a writer.

K: How do you feel about being a woman writer in the eighties?

E: It never crossed my mind that women were less than totally superior to men. My mother was the youngest of seven sisters, and all <u>their</u> men were outnumbered. Their men were frightfully nice, but background figures.

K: So you had a relatively different view, in fact feminist

without your realising it, of women coping and taking all the major decisions?

K: Did that help women become more independent?

E: Yes, it was perhaps more usual in my generation, as the men had to go off to fight in the Second World War.

K: Did that help women become more independent?

E: If you watch films of the thirties, you can see an independent woman emerging then, with her own car. After the war came the New Look, which ruined the image of women. My aunts were quite different from the housebound housewife. They went to the races, they smoked and they drank and went to the spit and sawdust part of the pub. I think the image of Marilyn Monroe has a lot to answer for.

K: So you think those who complain about women being captive in the home are only looking at a narrow range of middle-class women?

E: Yes certainly, I dislike the poor little me syndrome.

K: As a woman, do you feel limited by our language, as Angela Carter does?

E: No, not really. I don't quite understand what she means.

K: She's talking about the embarrassment of writing about certain women's issues, or perhaps fear of offending men.

E: Well, one can certainly never say everything one thinks to a man, even when one is very angry. All the women I talk to agree that men would be completely and utterly destroyed by some of the things we think about them.

K: We support their egos.

E: We feel compassion.

K: When you are writing novels, do you ever feel limited?

E: No, and I never rewrite. But I often have to make insertions, as the wretched novels are too short, sometimes by 100 pages.

K: Do you enjoy rereading them?

E: No, I can't bear it; my four boys don't read them.

K: But your husband does; he told me he likes your economical writing.

E: Well you don't want to keep nudging the reader. It's like not putting in too many stage directions, to leave space for the reader's imagination.

K: But it's other women writers you prefer to read?

E: Yes. Caroline Blackwood and especially Beryl Bainbridge. In fact I discovered her. She'd had two books published, by Macmillan I think. She lives round the corner and we both took our children to the local school.

K: I can see you're on the same wavelength. You must enjoy talking to each other?

E: Yes, I do tremendously. Then one day she showed me <u>Harriet Said</u> which had been in her agent's drawer for years, because so many people said it was disgusting. When I read it, I thought it was absolutely brilliant. So we published it at Duckworth's where I worked for five years.

K: It's your husband's firm, isn't it?

E: Yes, and beautifully easy to get to, in the Old Piano factory, just round the corner.

K: Your husband has a varied and interesting list - and now you and Beryl Bainbridge. What more are you experimenting with at the moment?

E: The first person, which can prove tough. I'd never done it before. If you happen to make up a person who is funny that's lovely. But if it's a boring person, I might get bored.

K: Do you hear them talking in your head?

E: Oh, yes, though I can't live with them as much as I want. I simply do what I can.

K: You've got the comic writer's perspective, so you can't live inside them as much as you want. Do you have difficulties with the endings?

E: I just like to see what happens. Though I'd thought out the ending more for <u>The Clothes and the Wardrobe</u>. Occasionally I use something that people have told me. It's like being in a boat, you have to be prepared to float. You have to be open to ideas, impressions.

K: That's interesting. Most writers find it difficult to describe their creative process fully.

E: Yes, an awful lot of it is mysterious and unconscious. You've got to listen to your unconscious. It's better not to face impressions immediately, but let them stew on the back burner so to speak. The stuff of art is like cooking. If you just rush things down, you merely produce journalism. Sometimes I feel like a medium when I'm writing a novel, as if it's not really me - does that sound phoney?

K: No, P.D. James said something similar. And I like your female image about stewing and cooking. Alice Walker talks of 'quilting' which is putting little bits together which others have discarded, to make something beautiful.

E: I was out in the street the other day when a wonderful idea occurred to me, but I couldn't write it down, and now it won't come back to me. I shall have to try and remember exactly what I was wearing and carrying and it might come back to me.

K: Do you keep notebooks?

E: No, just the backs of envelopes.

K: It seems to me that your novel writing is maturing, that you are planning them more.

E: It's interesting you should say that. When I got to the end of <u>The Clothes and the Wardrobe</u> I realised there was far more to say about the mother-in-law, so then I wrote a book from her point of view and now I'm on a third book about them.

K: How do you prefer to write? On a word-processor?

E: No, a felt tip pen, it leaves more space.

K: What advice have you got for people who are beginning to write?

E: You've got to be truthful, as Graham Greene said.

K: What does he mean?

E: He means that you've got to know who your characters

are; then you must not make them act out of character for the sake of the plot. It's difficult if you're writing in your own voice to give characters their own voices, because you're like a ventriloquist. I heard some excellent advice from a chap who teaches drama; he said 'I want you to write a scene between two people, say in Northern Ireland, between a Catholic and a Protestant; try to write it without anybody knowing whose side you are on.' That would be a brilliant test.

K: Do you take any notice of critics?

E: Some, if they have good advice.

K: You don't find criticism hurts?

E: No, I feel at a distance, fortunately. It's interesting, at the moment television is making a film of <u>Unexplained Laughter</u> with Elaine Page and Diana Rigg. I sat at the back the other day watching and felt it was more like a stepchild than my own creation.

K: Is any other book of yours to be filmed?

E: Perhaps <u>Clothes and the Wardrobe</u> - that should make some real money at last, if it comes off. The director will be a woman.

K: Do you enjoy the media aspect of being a well-known writer?

E: I don't like standing up in the evening and talking about my works, I feel such a bloody fool. I don't think any women do - except actresses, because it's their profession. Men don't seem to mind standing up and making speeches about the world.

K: We've not been taught to push ourselves forward.

E: I don't think we enjoy it. Look at any pub or gathering, darling. The men are holding forth 'This is what I think on this and that'. And the women don't get a look in. Then men have the cheek to say women talk too much. It's completely the reverse of the truth. When men come in to the office they allow women the odd word, that's all - or to put their lunch on the table.

K: Margaret Drabble considers that women novelists like yourself and Fay Weldon and Angela Carter are more interested in magic than men.

E: Yes, women take it more for granted. When they write about magic it's less about terrible beasts, such as the Great Beast 666. Women realise that the rational and the irrational are both in ourselves.

K: Do you mind about the way book prizes go?

E: I don't care a damn. And I never studied that whole area of English Literature.

K: So you come to writing fresher, with fewer forms or rules to follow. Are there bad days when you wonder why you write?

E: I often think it's a crazy thing to do. If I didn't do that I'd have to do something else to justify my existence.

K: Are there moments of real satisfaction?

E: It's more moments when the words go right. There's a sentence in Birds of the Air: I wrote that geese look like visions from some other reality, which they do. Geese are so amazing, so alive, so beautiful.

K: That's the novel of yours which I admired most.

E: I think I like it more than the others.

K: Alongside the humour you bring in the grief of a mother who has lost her only son. I have the impression you are now planning to include more of the inevitability of suffering, of that dark side of life.

E: I think I should do. I've just heard Anita Desai on television saying it's easier to link both in India, because nobody there expects a happy ending, so she feels freer to suggest the tragic side of life. I'd never go hunting for happy endings anyway.

K: Do you want to write any other kind of novel?

E: I want to try to do something like Mauriac. Something in neutral tones, without colour, to see if I could do it. Black and white, not much humour or description. I'd like to have a go at that.

K: But you're not a tormented Catholic?

E: Most of my family was Catholic. I was born in Liverpool.

K: So you might be a Catholic novelist, like Graham Greene. And do you share any of his methods of composition - always the same amount each day?

E: No, I sit making notes in the drawing room or the garden, and when the deadline looms I have to go away, to Wales. Rule 43.

K: When you felt you needed to express yourself, why didn't you do more paintings, since that's what you'd studied, and knew you were good at?

E: Painting is far more messy, far more concentrated, the children try to help you, the paint dries up.

K: But a novel is such an investment of time, surely?

E: A painting takes even more time.

K: Now that I'm looking at one of your paintings, I see what you mean. It is a fairly large portrait of one of your babies, with a family likeness which is impressive, and beautiful details in the embroidered clothes; it represents the individual - and it's an icon.

E: I'm glad you can see that, I try to do that when I'm painting, in fact I think it's something art should try to achieve.

K: Do you find time to paint nowadays?

E: No, but I used to paint whenever I wanted to capture something for myself, such as the faces of my children when they were small.

K: You obviously have a tremendous need to express your creativity. When your five children were younger, did you find that you could be creative through them?

E: Yes, frequently, making things that they wanted, such as slippers with eyes embroidered on them, or doing lots of things with them.

K: I'd like you to try to explain your almost miraculous and very ambitious choice of something as demanding as the novel when you first attempted writing.

E: It was as simple as thinking 'I've got something to say' - and saying it. It was as though you were stuck in a pub with everyone gassing away and you want to shout 'No it's not that way, this is the way I see it.'

K: So you were writing what you wanted to read and others weren't saying?

E: That's exactly it, absolutely. I painted because I wanted portraits of my children and couldn't afford to pay someone else.

K: It's not just that, it's because no one else could have caught them in quite your bold and turn-of-the-century style.

E: Well, you want to get something down and then you can embroider on it which is exactly what my painting's about.

K: Your writing embroiders less.

E: Books are an embroidery on the way you talk, aren't they?

K: I like that definition of a book: 'embroidery on the way you talk'.

E: It's formalising the whole thing.

K: It's also much more than that. You are giving your view of the world - which many people can then respond to. I loved your criticism of English weaknesses, that our icons are Winnie The Pooh Bear, the Queen, followed far behind by God. You must have spent time meditating on English foibles?

E: Not so much meditating as letting impressions sink down into the mud of your unconscious and fester there.

K: You see a false sentimentality, a misuse of energy.

E: I'll tell you what I feel like. I feel like somebody standing on a cliff screaming into the wind 'You've got it all wrong, it's not like that, it's more like this.'

K: That's a whole area of writing that I think extremely

important.

E: It's somewhat like preaching.

K: There is a prophetic element in Margaret Atwood, Emma Tennant and some of your comments, as when you criticise the 'politics of envy' or show the outsider teenager as being more sensible than his 'clever' parents in The Birds of the Air. You are writing social satire.

E: It's very difficult to know what is going on, yet somehow you realise everything is awry, everything is askew, and you don't know enough to analyse precisely what is going wrong. You don't know what you can say to make it go right, so you produce silly little novels just hinting at what could be going wrong.

K: Because we don't always appreciate humour, even judge it trivial, you underestimate what you are doing.

E: Well if you're a girl who left school at sixteen and didn't go to university, you feel diffident for a long time about saying 'Listen to me, you're mad.'

K: You are using humour to bring attention to our predicaments.

E: I think humour is terribly important. It's a wonderful weapon. Somewhere I said 'Evil and laughter cannot co-exist.'

K: I like that. In fact you satirise quite a range of topics. For example you sometimes poke fun at English love of emotional description of landscape. How consciously are you mocking the pathetic fallacy?

E: I love to do that. Like Stella Gibbons in Cold Comfort

Farm.

K: You do it magnificently, and much more concisely.

E: If I'd had the editing of that book, I'd have cut halfway through. I worked for five years as editor, and did a wonderful job helping writers.

K: So you were like the nineteenth-century editor, advising on writing. You've obviously had wide experience judging what works in fiction.

E: I could tell when they were getting off their track. Today nobody even seems to copy edit properly - or they send your MS to a child from Oxford.

K: At this stage I don't suppose you allow anyone to change your MS?

E: My husband is allowed to say if something is ungrammatical, that's all.

K: Your ideas seem to be getting bigger, even including the voices of the dead in Unexplained Laughter.

E: I'll tell you about that: I wanted to write that book as the spirit of Wales. Then I thought 'No you can't do that; have the voice of a dead child.' The point about Wales is that the landscape is so compelling, so beautiful, magical. Every landscape I describe is inspired by Wales. When I'm there I do see visions - the landscape is a sort of vision. I even hear voices; I woke up one night, I was on my own, and I heard these friendly voices downstairs, so I thought 'Hang on darling, don't disturb.'

K: Yes, your voices are neither frightening nor menacing. How do they do them in the film?

E: One girl is a voice-over, another the girl who appears. And Diana Rigg is Lydia, Elaine Page is Betty.

K: Tell me more about <u>Twenty-Seventh Kingdom</u>.

E: I'd made up Valentine almost completely, though she's also based on a nurse from South Africa. I'd met some Jamaicans who told me all about Jamaica, the food, the Jonkanoo. I put in a girl called Joan because I'd known one in the Lake District. Then Nancy Banks Smith wrote an article in the <u>Guardian</u> about the obituary column in the Jamaican newspaper <u>Daily Gleaner</u> - how most of the names were so extraordinary, like Florizel Glasspole, and then there was a Joan. How on earth did that peculiar coincidence occur? I've had such weird coincidences in my life that I've been forced to take another look at the universe. When ghosts and coincidences happen, you just accept them at first; then later you reflect on the fact that it's a spiritual experience. Your unconscious has processed them.

eva

figes

EVA FIGES was born in Berlin in April 1932, but has lived most of her life in London.

Novels	Equinox (1966)
	Winter Journey (1967)
	Konek Landing (1969)
	Days (1974)
	Nelly's Version (1977)
	Waking (1981)
	Light (1984)
	The Seven Ages (1986)
	Ghosts (1988)
Radio Plays	Time Regained (1980)
	Days (from her novel, 1981)
Non Fiction	Patriarchal Attitudes: Women in Society (1970)
	Tragedy and Social Revolution (1976)
	Little Eden: A Child at War (autobiography, 1978)
	Sex and Subterfuge (1982)
As Editor	Classic Choice 1 (1965)
	Modern Choice 1 & 2 (1965-66)
	Women Their World (with Abigail Mozley & Dinah Livingstone, 1980)
Juvenile	The Muscians of Bremen: Retold (1967)
	The Banger (1968)
	Scribble Sam (1971)

K: Your name was first made by <u>Patriarchal Attitudes</u> published in 1970. It's a study of the way male writers have excluded, marginalised, undervalued or vilified women, from the Greeks to the present day. You point out how writers, considered revolutionary or liberating, often had the opposite effect on women, such as Rousseau and Freud. Did it take long to research that book?

F: I was writing a novel at the same time, and only researching in the afternoons. Once I'd decided what I was looking for, it was easy. The main problem was to get a framework. Having decided what it was going to be, I looked for evidence. I hadn't read much Rousseau before that, but I knew that Mary Wollstonecraft objected to his ideas. She wrote the <u>Vindication</u> in answer to Rousseau. He's such a key figure politically that I started looking at many key figures and found similar sexual prejudices.

K: In all of them?

F: That was central to my argument: that every important figure had similar prejudice against women. It didn't take too long to establish that.

K: I thought it must have taken some time, you use such beautiful images, from the very first page, such as women having to dance in a mirror held by men.

F: Thanks, but that's because I'm a writer. I started saying we have to look on culture as male culture and not as shared. The whole of our culture has been made by men. If one starts with that assumption, my hunch would be that it always shows a bias as a result. Nobody had quite examined 'great' writers such as Schopenhauer and Darwin in that way and I found bias almost invariably there. It's rare to find heroes without it. The much vaunted male logic isn't logical, because they display prejudices - against half the human race - that are considered prejudices according to any dictionary definition.

K: Since your book there has been some fascinating feminist literary criticism, first in America and now here. What do you think of Ellen Moer's <u>Literary Women</u> and Elaine Showalter's <u>A Literature of Their Own</u>?

F: It's very interesting, and I've done some myself in <u>Sex and Subterfuge</u>. However, I don't agree with much that they say because their feminism has overruled some literary values, which are paramount to me. I don't think you are doing women a favour simply by listing everybody who happens to have written a book and happens to be a woman.

K: What they are doing is more sociological than you.

F: But many of the reissues of older novels are second rate, not great.

K: Some are disappointing; but they have helped us revalue Edith Wharton, Willa Cather and realise that there is a women's tradition, that had been subsumed into the 'malestream'. Each time women started to write, they had to start afresh. You helped too, making us look again at novelists of the eighteenth century like Fanny Burney.

F: In this country women have changed the whole course of the English novel, since Jane Austen; Maria Edgeworth influenced Scott, a male giant. That influence is too often forgotten. But I don't like the idea of a ghetto of women's writing, I wanted to emphasise that women had done something important <u>in</u> the British literary tradition.

K: Feminists also point out a continuity of those who were perhaps not the greatest, but writing as well as men who were more favourably reviewed.

F: That's true. Even if some of these women were not worth reprinting in the last analysis, how many men are worthy of the attention they receive? It has a lot to do with our critical tradition, and so many critics are men.

K: That's beginning to change.

F: At professional level they are still mainly men. A few years ago I looked at examination papers. Not only were there very few women writers at degree level, there were very few on the 'A' level syllabus, which is more crucial. If there was a woman she was shoved into a 'genre' category. Many of the topics exclude women, for example 'War' automatically excludes us. Many papers did not offer a single woman writer. Even today it's only 10 per cent.

K: You came to England at the age of seven, speaking only German. What did the learning of a new language make you aware of?

F: It made me aware that there are very different ways of saying things. And it gave me an interest in words, which I have never lost.

K: Do you still write in German?

F: No, but I speak it fluently, well enough to interview Gunther Grass. I seldom write in German because the structures would force me to write quite differently. In fact when Gombrich was asked to translate his Story of Art back into his native German, he said he couldn't do it, as German grammatical structures would make it into a different book.

K: The awareness of two languages encouraged you to turn to poetry at school. When did you begin writing novels?

F: Not till my late twenties. I read English Literature at university, married young and when the children went to playschool, found myself with a little spare time. Middle-class women at home feel they can turn to writing as it's been considered a reputable occupation for them since the nineteenth century. My first novel Equinox was published in the mid 1960s.

K: Your second novel Winter Journey was well reviewed, I think?

F: Yes, Robert Nye praised my 'empathy for the impotence of extreme age found in Beckett's finest writing.'

K: He coined the phrase 'the poetry of the inarticulate' for your achievement in that brief novel. Why didn't you continue in that vein?

F: After the first two I wanted to branch out a little. I'd begun working in an office, but wanted to write social and literary criticism. I was fortunate in starting to write for the Guardian's women's page, where I produced mainly think-pieces for its editor, Mary Stott. I remember writing on topics such as Equal Pay, which made me feel somewhat angry. I started my first non-fiction book Patriarchal Attitudes because I felt angry and wanted to change people's attitudes.

K: Have your views changed much since that book was published?

F: Not fundamentally; though many other feminists have, and consider me somewhat old-fashioned these days.

K: When did you begin to write?

F: When I was a schoolgirl, I wanted to be a writer then
- I thought I was going to be a poet - and even then I
was aware that I had other faculties which I thought
might get in the way of poetry. Of course, in a sense
it doesn't, because you need that critical sense as a
novelist as well, but I have on the whole tended to
divide up my activity in those two ways. I find that
non-fiction writing is a great release because it's so
easy for me; once you've done your homework and got
your facts rights, it's like putting a knife through
butter.

K: Do the two kinds of writing give you a different
relationship to the real world?

F: Yes, and that's one of the reasons why I've written
non-fiction. I've usually been motivated by a sense of
anger or outrage or impatience with things and I want
to make other people see it.

K: So there's a clear political function to your non-
fiction?

F: Oh yes. Very much so. I was clear when I wrote
Patriarchal Attitudes that I was writing polemic, I
wasn't writing an academic book and it had a function
as polemic. I had to batten down the hatches and
make sure I didn't leave any loopholes because I was
trying to press home an argument in the most effective
way.

K: So what is different when you write a novel?

F: Well, in the first instance it's a much more intuitive
thing. Instead of rationally picking your topic because
that's what you think needs doing, with a novel, your
topic picks you, it chooses you. You may start with an

image or some tiny incident or some vague anecdote and things focus around it; if they don't, then the idea's no good and it stops itself. You're partly discovering things about yourself.

K: Do you think your non-fiction books about women have helped your fiction writing?

F: I think with hindsight that my rational, non-fiction writing has in fact reconditioned me at the intuitive level; I was brought up to accept certain things about my own gender, or at least to take them in and only protest at a very subliminal level, but this process of writing polemical stuff - which after all is an education to oneself as well as to everyone else - has affected the way I write about women in my fiction, and I see that now. For example, in my early novels I tended to concentrate most of my energy into my male characters.

K: What happened after you'd written <u>Patriarchal Attitudes</u>?

F: I started taking female characters much more centrally; things that I was repressing or keeping in the background in order to keep them under control were then able to come out. I suppose it was a question of understanding - that once you understand a problem from every angle then you don't have this danger of things getting out of hand, which can ruin a novel; and I did feel that if I was going to have a woman character she would inevitably become me and that was not on. Though if you take a man as a character, it is an aspect of yourself anyway. In the novel I've just finished I found it was far easier to identify with the male characters, because it's set in 1900 and when you think of the social inhibitions on women at that time, it is actually very hard to put yourself imaginatively into it.

K: Do you think there's a difference in the male and female imagination?

F: Only in so far as their experience is different, which it often is. There are certain images which are frequently connected with women in fiction, such as the house. This has been a potent image for two hundred years.

K: You discuss it in Sex and Subterfuge.

F: Yes, there's quite a lot in that book. I examined where the house is used in Gothic fiction. And since the eighteenth century by novelists including Jane Austen in Mansfield Park. Think of the very titles such as Wuthering Heights, The Tenant of Wildfell Hall.

K: In recent novels too?

F: They are potent images in my own fiction. I tend to focus on a house as I did in Light, where I use Monet's own house and garden. Virginia Woolf does it too, think of Mrs Ramsay's house. It has something to do with women's experience, with their emotional nexus associated with the house which men don't appear to have in fiction in the same way.

K: Surely feminist fiction would use the enclosing image less?

F: I don't read much of it, but I think that self-consciously feminist fiction is hampering itself by taking off, being propagandist. It tends to be realist, as Zoe Fairbairns's novels can be - which can limit the imagination. I experiment with different forms when writing about female experience.

K: I much admire your novel Waking, about seven stages in a woman's life, through the perceptions of her body - and emotions. It seemed to me that you were using stream-of-consciousness to convey her teaming thoughts. You exploit its qualities without allowing the fragmentary sentence structure to alienate the reader.

F: John Berger wrote an essay on that, saying it's not stream-of-consciousness, as a child would not have that vocabulary. But in a sense, though a child does not possess those words, he does have those perceptions. You have to get a certain narrative technique for each book. Once I'd decided to limit it to the moment of waking in the morning, which I did for deliberate reasons. I had to evolve a style that did not fit the categories of realism or modernism. Stream-of-consciousness has always been an artificial device, it's never been realistic as otherwise it would have been extremely tedious and boring.

K: As so many of our thoughts are. I wondered precisely how you were working at the style while you were writing, as I think you have forged a magnificent discourse for shifting from the conscious to the subconscious, from a physical to an ethereal image, sometimes in the same sentence.

F: To be honest, I don't remember worrying much about that. Once I'd found the form, which took me a long time, I realised 'This is what I want.' In fact it was one of the few times that felt like inspiration. Then I didn't worry about narrative techniques, which seemed to follow. The essential was to find the form: the idea of waking up in the early morning. I knew I wanted something very intimate. I'd tried various experiments, such as writing in diary form, which I discovered to be very unsatisfactory.

K: Why? Wasn't it intimate enough?

F: No, it turned out flat and mundane.

K: I'm interested that you use the word 'inspiration'.
Writers like Dorothy Richardson spoke of an almost
passive awareness when they were writing - just
being receptive. Do you find your subconscious working
even more than your conscious mind?

F: Yes. There is this passive element. You can't worry
at something - well you can try, but it doesn't work out
logically. You have to wait if necessary. On the other
hand before I wrote Waking I certainly destroyed
page after page. I went through a very bad patch for
six months, and then got to a turning point. In a sense
it's naive to call that inspiration, after pacing the floor
for weeks. After that I was still unsure of myself and
didn't even keep a copy in order not to tempt providence.

K: You write straight onto a typewriter?

F: Yes, usually with carbon copy, even of first draft. But
I was so afraid I might tear this up too.

K: Your approach reminds me of what Virginia Woolf
said about the female space being inner consciousness;
that we have a superiority in understanding this area
better than most men. Even if you don't agree with
her, it's the area you are most interested in.

F: There is subconscious intuition at work when you are
writing creatively, and you must listen to that. The
best writers of any sex must do that. Perhaps women
are more able to trust that area, than many men.

K: Because they live with it more?

F: If it's true; of course men are taught to trust their
reason which isn't much help when you're creating a
work of art. Obviously reason comes in, the rational
ability which judges, stands aside or corrects. However,
male writers like Flaubert and Proust trusted their

inner judgement and intuition rather than logical intelligence. At gestation stage you don't always know <u>why</u> you want to follow a particular trail.

K: But you know some of the reasons why?

F: At a deeper level you don't, and that's the more interesting level. Sometimes there's no logical reason why you decide to put something in or not; it's a gut level which determines what's appropriate.

K: Yet your novels are so finely structured.

F: I like the idea of form. It's a discipline and it gives you a structure.

K: When does that come?

F: At the beginning. I start with the shape, the idea of a new form.

K: While writing, were you influenced by word associations?

F: I don't think so because that could be dangerous. You could drift off, be led astray. It's a short book, concentrating a great deal of experience. I was interested in the relationship to one's own body.

K: Virginia Woolf said a woman could never tell the whole truth about her own body. Was it still a problem for you to find suitable discourse?

F: What I wanted to convey is what it's like being inside a female body; in a sense the fact that it's female is unimportant; it's merely my body. I think Woolf had a problem as she had so many physical and sexual hangups. We are probably less inhibited nowadays.

K: I see you within the tradition of impressionism, yet not limited by it. Woolf could not suggest that Mrs Dalloway or Mrs Ramsay had a sex life, whereas you convey powerfully what it's like to be pregnant, for instance.

F: That's a limitation of Woolf herself as a person. She had no children, she was frigid, so there were whole areas of experience cut off.

K: However you use notions which are similar, such as her insistence that consciousness is a semi-transparent halo, life not going from 'gig lamp to gig lamp' as she put it. Very few people followed up what she was doing with impressionism, after The Waves. There was a hiatus until you carried on, overcoming some of her problems.

F: It's interesting you should say that. Before writing Waking I reread The Waves. I remembered it as a fascinating experiment which did not actually succeed. It can be used in the sense that one could learn both from where she failed as well as where she succeeded. I liked the form she used, the six disembodied voices. Though they are not different people at all, the six voices are just one person. And the physical dimension is completely missing. After all, like language, nature is also a form of sensuous experience, and it's vital, missing in her intellectual approach. I did partially use her as a model.

K: I felt you did, but wanted to hear how. She developed it into a female aesthetic, how far do you agree with her on that?

F: We still don't know how much gender differences are a matter of conditioning. Men have tended to use the novel differently; partly for ambition, and needing to make a living. The commercialism that creeps into much male writing dictates the way many write. What they regard as important topics in life, like war and peace and power obviously help to frame the novels they produce.

K: But you've got to make money too. Or can you put your aesthetic considerations first more frequently than many male writers?

F: There is a whole nexus of considerations: not all women write like me, indeed few do. I love language above all, and first wanted to be a poet.

K: At the moment novels dealing with social and political issues are talked of more. Isn't yours a lonely furrow?

F: <u>Light</u> is selling well in America, where experiments are accepted more favourably. But I don't think one has much choice - the topic chooses one. It's a question of <u>what</u> one has to say. I'd write more books like <u>Patriarchal Attitudes</u> if I wanted to examine social problems. Social novels tend to suggest there's some sort of solution, whereas I write about areas where there is no simple solution.

K: Such as having to live inside one's own body. Could you have used a male body in <u>Waking</u>? You end with fear of ageing, fairly universal.

F: When you are writing with that degree of intimacy, it's better to use a body you know well. Furthermore, the female body has a cycle which gives a satisfying structure, rising to the climax of childbirth. Writing as a man would have put up false barriers.

K: Like Beckett, you don't name your woman.

F: I often don't name my characters, you don't need a name when you sleep. Anyway, I don't believe in character, I think it's a misleading concept.

K: Is your view more Buddhist?

F: I take an Aristotelian view, that it's by our actions we are happy or unhappy. I think that the situation is important and how people behave in that situation. The idea of character is a myth.

K: Nathalie Sarraute thought 'character' is putting on useless labels.

F: She's right. You then get into the area of caricature, like Dickens, whose people are quaint, or grotesque. They may be irrelevant to the situation you're interested in.

K: You are more interested in archetypal situations, like the adolescent thinking about how adults behave.

F: Character can be a falsification. But in <u>Light</u> I'm dealing with real people, which set up many problems. I was lucky in that many of them correspond to categories, such as 'old man', 'young child'.

K: I was fascinated by <u>Light</u>. You chose Monet and his family, evoking them through the perceptions of each of the family in turn.

F: I had to flesh each one out, guess at them in turn. But I didn't want readers to think immediately of Monet, so I call him Claude. I don't want people to read with biographical preconceptions, which might disappoint.

K: Why did you break so completely from the nineteenth-century novel?

F: For me it had always been a well-structured continuous narrative and I suddenly realised that life is not like that. When I looked back on my life, I saw isolated images in my head. It was that realisation that made it possible for me to start writing novels. I said to myself 'I'll write something which is just fragments, strung together;' and in fact my first prose work, which was never published, was just that, isolated memories strung together, with no connecting narrative at all. They were just put on the page, with gaps in between. But of course the moment you've done that you can't stay there, you begin to evolve something else. Therefore the next thing I did, which was my first published book, used that same technique, but by now I was very subtly telling a story and even though the gaps were still on the page, any reader would immediately connect one thing with another.

K: What made you so sure the reader would immediately connect the gaps on your page?

F: I don't think very much about the reader. In that first book I did make certain concessions which I wouldn't make again. I threw in a little bit of action, because I knew what would happen if I didn't - in other words that it would get nowhere.

K: What if the reader believes that life is lived in consecutive chapters? Are you working towards a sense of order?

F: I don't think that sense of order comes from within. Though I believe that the plot - crude word - is something that actually comes to you and you don't choose. It's like a seed blown in the window, which settles and doesn't go away along with the petals; then you know this is the real thing after a bit; it chooses itself in a way. Because you work at two different levels at the same time. There is one level which knows what you're about and why, and there's another level where there are subconscious forces at work that make you choose that theme. It's only after you've written it, that it becomes clear why that particular theme.

K: Do you ever start with plot?

F: I don't even like that word. I rarely start with plot though I often end with one. Life does not narrate, but you end up narrating anyway.

K: How do you connect your beginnings with your endings?

F: You make up a different kind of story. The old-fashioned kind of plot is a hindrance. I can think of one novel - my third - which had a strong story line. I thought 'this is easy, it tells itself'. But after two drafts I felt extremely unhappy because you get a kind of separation between the story itself and the ways you tell it. To me the way you tell something, the story and the style are more important than what you are saying. I had a phase when I wrote far more simply and concentrated on exposing the inherent ambiguities of the story itself.

K: Not unlike the <u>nouveau roman</u>, the new type of French novel of 60s and 70s?

F: Yes, in the sense that the reader was perpetually having to question what was actually happening. I wrote a novel about a woman with amnesia - <u>Nelly's Version</u>. On one level it has all the conventional narrative techniques of people and characters but of course is used quite differently to expose the very fiction. The whole purpose of this amnesia is for the woman to make a new start; but there's no such thing as a new start, everything repeats itself. The very fact that she's amnesiac, and that she's amnesiac for a purpose, and telling her story, throws the story into a different perspective from the kind of realist narrative which we're used to.

K: Is the novel withdrawing into itself or is it the narrator?

F: The novel in the twentieth century ought to be going in this direction, in the sense that reportage, in various forms, is so much better done on film and television. It's the novel which can reproduce the ambiguity in one's own mind, the subjective viewpoint. I often use someone in a psychological crisis, because the novel can do this better than any other form. And when one is actually writing, it all takes place in one's head. The conventional novel with a third person narrator presents only a selective version of the truth, a tiny fraction. It's what goes on in people's heads and how they see the world that is just as important as the colour of the traffic lights - in fact more so.

K: But surely modern novels telling stories can say something new?

F: There's a sense in which <u>Dr Zhivago</u> is saying the same thing as <u>War and Peace</u> because it is using exactly the same techniques to tell exactly the same kind of story a hundred years later. I would reject that, we know all about war and peace from Tolstoy. We now want something else in the novel.

K: Which writers have influenced you most this century?

F: Proust and Virginia Woolf. But as I only came to England at seven, I've tended to look more abroad than most English writers. My outlook from the start has been more European than British. In German I read and admire Gunther Grass especially.

K: You have the advantage of being able to interview him in German. Do you also like the east German novelist

Krista Wolf?

F: I like <u>Krista K</u> her first, the autobiographical novel. I feel uneasy with her other works, she seems evasive.

K: Which women writing at the moment do you think most interesting?

F: I don't read them while I'm writing. In England, Angela Carter.

K: She's very different from you, using feminism explicitly.

F: She's self-consciously literary, and her allusions seem strange to me, so they intrigue me. I liked the one book I read by the American Marilyn Robinson. Kathy Acker is interesting as she's doing something which nobody has done before, and only a woman can do. Of course I admire Doris Lessing, but think she ought to craft her forms more. I don't have time to read contemporaries widely; in fact, one picks and chooses according to one's needs. Sometimes you're reading past writers, sometimes no fiction, but researching for other books. At the moment I'm writing a historical novel.

K: I find that surprising, as it demands plot and character.

F: <u>Light</u> was a historical novel in its modest way. I suspect the real reason is because one is running out of experiences. The sort of writing I've done till now demanded personal responses. Having reached middle age, I feel one comes to a time when one's psychic life is virtually over. You've gone through all the stages of love, marriage, children, divorce, hope, disappointment.

K: Now you're looking outside?

F: Yes. In a way the broadening scope is refreshing.

K: One of the advantages of being alive today is that we can have a second life at our age. Charlotte Bronte felt really old at thirty.

F: As long as you can cope; but there are problems if you expect it to continue in the same sort of way. It's humbling to think how young so many writers died in the past, when one reflects on how little one has achieved.

K: Which feminist theorist do you find most interesting?

F: I've heard Dale Spender talking and I think what she says about man-made language is valuable - though God knows what the solution is. Patriarchal use of language is so basic, so pervasive.

K: I think it helps a little to say 'human being' instead of 'man'.

F: Yes, but it's got to come naturally.

K: Have you found it a problem?

F: It's always a problem, at a basic technical level, because unless you want to write every time 's/he' then you are in a bind, and you write clumsily or have a sex bias. It's not a problem in fiction. I feel that fundamentally all women writers must write about an experience that <u>all</u> human beings can identify with, including men. Some of my most intimate books men have responded to. Men can identify with <u>Waking</u> and <u>Days</u>. In a sense they are about female experience. But at a fundamental level, if it's true, then it's almost always true for men as well as women.

K: Isn't there prejudice to be overcome?

F: You see that in the reviews; there are men who say 'I don't understand this.' Or they dismiss it; but other men respond positively. However I sometimes feel men and women are drifting more apart, because women are not writing so much to please men, but themselves.

K: Like Fay Weldon?

F: Yes, and why should they please men when 50 per cent of the population consists of women? Why should you ingratiate yourself with the other sex if they don't want to know? There is a tendency at the moment, if you talk of women's experience, for men to be turned off by it. This is often their loss. At a more discriminating level, men say 'I can recognise myself in this' - if a book is truthful, not propagandist.

To a great extent, every writer has to remake language. It's one of the first things you have to do. You have to remake language to find a voice of your own. A particular woman may find particular problems. But in my experience the innate male bias is there in non-fiction rather than novel writing. Every time you write 'one' or 's/he' to stop people mentally excluding women, you become clumsy. There are so many words which have a sex bias. How many years has Margaret Thatcher been in power? Yet whenever I hear 'prime minister' I have a masculine image.

K: You are often included in the group of experimental novelists who have discarded plot and characterisation, Alan Burns, Gabriel Josipovici, Alan Johnson, as you all radically questioned what held the novel together. In your nine novels you have gradually refined ways of conveying how our thoughts and feelings live uneasily together. Your heart moves in with your head to let thought processes come to life. Will you continue with non-fiction or will you concentrate on novel writing?

F: I suspect I've written my last non-fiction book. I don't really care to give opinions any more; I've given my opinion on the things I feel most strongly about - women and literature - and I feel that fiction is now what's most important. I think that in the non-fiction I was fulfilling a role more as a citizen, and in the novels as an artist. I now feel that I want to function as an artist, and it's time for other people to change the world if they're ever going to. For what it's worth I've done my little bit. My time is running out and so it has become too valuable. I think perhaps that it's also because I'm more confident about the fiction; I'm getting better at it and therefore it takes more out of me; it's therefore more worthwhile giving everything to it.

nadine

gordimer

NADINE GORDIMER was born in Springs in the
Transvaal of South Africa in November 1923.

Novels	The Lying Days (1953) A World of Strangers (1958) Occasion for Loving (1963) The Late Bourgeois World (1966) A Guest of Honour (1970) The Conservationist (1974) Burger's Daughter (1979) July's People (1981)

Short Stories	Face to Face: Short Stories (1949)
	The Soft Voice of the Serpent and
	    Other Stories (1952)
	Six Feet of the Country (1956)
	Friday's Footprints and Other Stories
	    (1960)
	Not for Publication and Other Stories
	    (1965)
	Penguin Modern Stories 4 (with
	    others, 1970)
	Livingstone's Companions: Stories
	    (1971)
	Selected Stories (1975)
	Some Monday for Sure (1976)
	A Soldier's Embrace (1980)

Other	South African Writing Today (editor,
	    with Lionel Abrahams, 1967)
	African Lit. (lectures, University of
	    Cape Town, 1972)
	On the Mines (photographs by David
	    Goldblatt, 1973)
	The Black Interpreters: Notes on
	    African Writing (1973)

K: 'I never read a book as a child in which I myself was recognisable' says one of your characters in <u>The Lying Days</u>. Was that your experience as a child growing up in South Africa?

G: Yes, though emotionally there were books that had relevance to my life. D.H. Lawrence was a great favourite of mine when I was fifteen. His wonderful feeling for nature, the face of a pansy, a little tortoise, all these things he wrote about were marvellous and I could relate to them. The South African landscape is sensuous, so I could respond to his sensuousness. But everything else is totally different.

K: What are some of the obvious differences?

G: The seasons. When I was a small child, brought up on Angela Brazil and Dickens and so on, all the festive occasions were celebrated at the wrong seasons. My books had snow and robins, while we were out picnicking at Christmas.

K: That's an experience shared by Australians and New Zealanders.

G: Yes, and when I began reading Katherine Mansfield, I realised here was somebody who was writing about this other world, whose seasons at least I shared. Then I understood it was possible to be a writer even if you didn't live in Europe.

K: Did you come from a literary background?

G: No, not at all. My father was a shopkeeper. He had a small shop where he sold jewelry. He sold commemorative canteens of cutlery for retiring mine managers and engagement and wedding rings and watches. My mother didn't work, very few women seemed to then in South Africa. She was a great reader, at a popular level.

K: So you have her to thank for your love of books?

G: She made sure she read to me and my sister every night. And when I was five years old, she joined the local municipal library. There I felt like a pig in clover. Nobody tried to direct what I was reading. I've often reflected since on the significance of something like that in a country like South Africa. Had I been a black child I would not have been allowed to go to that library and might never have become a writer.

K: Why did you have a few years off school?

G: When I was eleven I developed a very slight heart ailment. My mother, being unhappily married, reacted in a way that many women like that do: she clung tremendously to her children. As my sister was older, and went away, to become a teacher, I was left at home. My mother seized on this illness as a way to keep me near her.

K: You mention a mother not unlike yours in The Termitary published in 1974.

G: Yes. My mother took me out of school till I was fourteen, a big slice out of a child's life. She took me to a women who taught me for a couple of hours a day. I absolutely hated it, as I was all alone with this woman. There's nothing more lonely. When I think of Victorian children with tutors, I realise what it must have been like for them. I discovered later that I should never have been taken out of school. But she did it, and I was alone a great deal. It was then that I began to write.

K: Did you have a good relationship with your mother?

G: It was a very loving relationship at the beginning, and <u>much</u> too dependent. This made me very careful not to allow my children to become too dependent upon me. I realised that the best thing you can do for your children is to set them free. Of course like everybody else, I haven't always succeeded. I've done my children damage in some ways. One isn't perfect. But I have succeeded, since they were quite small, in making them independent, in not overprotecting them. The cruellest thing you can do is to make a child defenceless.

K: As a child, did you long to go to Europe?

G: When I made the heroine in my first novel go to Europe it was a kind of wish fulfilled, I wanted to go to Europe but never had the opportunity to do so. That was the time when we thought literature, culture, art was abroad, you couldn't do it where you were. Of course we were quite wrong, you can be a writer anywhere, so I can't see any advantage in leaving. Some who are greatly talented have continued to develop in exile. But they do not write the books they would if they stayed. I'm not saying it's a disaster - look at Doris Lessing. But I know of so many others who have left at a point where exile became stultifying, because of a fragility in themselves or their personalities or their talent.

K: You stayed in Johannesburg. How did you start writing?

G: Writing short stories when I was a child. I published my first story, my first adult story, when I was fifteen, in a small journal in South Africa.

K: Did you find you had to invent a new language to write about what <u>you</u> saw round you, but didn't find in European books?

G: I didn't find it necessary to invent a special language. There was a problem with some words which mean something to us in South Africa, but no one outside, such as 'donga' for ditch, and names of plants and birds. It's up to the writer to make it intelligible, so that the reader can respond, make the leap, in his or her mind. I was used to reading novels of the deep south in America, and didn't mind not knowing what a 'judas tree' was, and not recognising how they speak.

K: That didn't make you feel left out?

G: I suppose my experience was that of any white person in a colonial situation beginning to write - that literature was somewhere else. As a child the books had such a distinct physical atmosphere. I was unconscious of the really important things.

K: You mean the social situation? Were you aware of what was happening in South Africa?

G: No, I don't think so. When you're a child your parents are your models. Their life seems the only possible life and you take on their attitudes. You only begin to question and rebel against them when you become a teenager.

K: But you went to the local school?

G: I went to the local convent school, where every child was white. We had a black servant, a woman who looked after us all my childhood, and who was too often looked on as an appendage. Now I feel deeply ashamed of being told not to accept drinks in her little room. My mother said her cups might be dirty, but at the time no servants were given hot water in their rooms, nor allowed baths. I didn't even know if she had a child or not. Of course I saw the black children who used to play in the street. It didn't occur to me that it was strange they couldn't come to my school, nor come to Saturday matinees at the cinema. It seemed a God-given rule. It was only later that I began to <u>see</u> and question.

K: You said not long ago that the short story you wrote when you were eighteen 'Ah Woe is me' is one of the first that showed some sense of the political situation?

G: It's about a white woman and her relationship with a former Black servant. I had been moving in an unconscious way to the real issues of my country. When I began to question it was on the level of someone who had always had a black servant. I often think that if I'd been Black I couldn't have become a writer. The library was only for whites, and as my parents were not rich we had few books in the house. I'd ask for books as presents for Christmas and my birthday and look forward to them for the whole year, and save up pocket money to buy books.

K: What led you to turn from short fiction to your first novel? It wasn't published till you were thirty.

G: I had wanted to write a novel since my late teens and made several attempts, but didn't like what I wrote. It occurred to me later that I hadn't lived enough, that my life was too constricted.

K: In fact <u>The Lying Days</u> is an autobiographical novel, one of the most moving I've read about a girl growing up.

G: It's my only autobiographical novel. I felt my life was too narrow emotionally; but I could use small striking incidents, that could be contained, like an egg. A short story is like an egg, it's all there. Whereas when I write a novel, it's an unknown territory, and it takes time to move from one territory to anther. I began to write that novel when I was about twenty-five.

K: It seems to me a novel primarily about emotional growth. I didn't notice at first that the 1949 Nationalist government was an important factor in the heroine's growing up. She's aware of its importance and of the slowness of the changes which affect whites.

G: She said it takes a long time for changes to permeate. I don't think the novel reflects adequately what that election meant. My preoccupations were still very personal and adolescent, as so often happens in first novels. At the end the heroine decides to come back from abroad, though for a time she had felt, like Hemingway's generation, that you couldn't be a writer or painter right where you lived, but had to go off to Paris. Now people feel quite the contrary, that exile is deprivation.

K: In The Lying Days you wrote that 'a guilt had began working on me. like a hairshirt.' The next two novels you wrote do seem to me to be more and more about the way politics affect personal life.

 I loved World of Strangers when I first discovered it. You show implicitly that the white heroine, and the black hero, who never meet, are basically similar in their desire to live through the senses, and not worry about politics. In Occasion for Loving you chose to write about a black and white love affair. One of the characters talks about how the personal is driven back to the social in South Africa, the political is personal, whether you like it or not. How conscious were you of that in your own life?

G: Very much so. By the time I wrote that book I was living in Johannesburg and mixing in a very different milieu from the mining town. By that time I had black friends as well as white. You must remember it was a time of great political turmoil. You had the great 'defiance' campaign. I did not take part, I was rather slow to develop politically but I was tremendously aware of this ferment around me, in people whose lives affected mine, and were involved.

K: The first novel of yours where the protagonist is really political is <u>The Late Bourgeois World</u>. It's about a divorced woman who doesn't do much politically, she just makes available an aunt's bank account.

G: That's a momentous decision, a big and dangerous decision.

K: That was the beginning of something for her?

G: Yes it was. Like all writers who don't seek exotic locations, who work from within their own society, whatever is changing in that society will come into the work. That kind of agonising decision was coming to people. The preoccupations of my first novel are being bypassed, belong to a different era. The historical connections between fiction and fact are stronger than we often think. It may not be conscious in the writer's mind, but it's always there.

K: <u>Berger's Daughter</u> is your novel which tackles head on what was happening in South Africa in the seventies - and whites working together with blacks.

G: It was the only novel that had any motive other than the desire to write simply what I knew. It was an act of homage to people like Rosa Berger's family. By that time I had become fascinated and amazed by such people. It's an act of homage to the amazing, astonishing, extraordinarily brave people who were prepared to devote their whole lives to the cause they saw was right. I had been waiting for someone inside that milieu to write about them. But it happened mainly in non-fiction, memoirs. I've always believed there are so many inhibitions in the most honest autobiographical work that even if they want to reveal themselves, they cannot reveal others, or hurt them too much. In fiction you are free to put what you know of fact in an imaginary form.

K: It's a painful story because Rosa spends so much time trying to escape that political heritage.

G: I was fascinated by the topic as I had teenage children myself by that time. You watch your children get to the stage when they break away; sometimes it's done easily, depending on the parents and the children; sometimes it's a painful and difficult process on both sides. I see something amazing in families which are totally politically dedicated, they carry on from generation to generation. It's like a strong genetic strain. Very often the children and grandchildren take up the torch.

K: But it's also about the problems of blacks working alongside whites?

G: In the seventies it was becoming an issue because you had the growth of Black Consciousness; black liberation movements had been banned and were working with great difficulty underground. There was an unhappily dormant time till Black Consciousness built up a sense of identity, and began to inspire black people with a sense of being themselves. This meant a drawing away from whites. There was also a feeling that there had been a failure of liberal motivation for change. If you don't succeed it doesn't matter how much you've done, you don't count any more. White liberalism had not achieved the ending of apartheid, it did not meet the historical demands of the time.

K: Rosa's parents were not liberals, but radicals.

G: They had worked closely with blacks. Rosa Berger grew up during the separation, and is rejected by the black child she was brought up with. In fact that's what makes her want to travel abroad for a time.

K: Have you ever lost your hope for a peaceful revolution in South Africa?

G: Even before the UDS existed, I had never lost my belief in the eventual future of a good and decent society, more just - though not utopia.

K: But you've also said that you feel more and more sympathy with Turgenev.

G: Yes, so much in him pertains to subjects I've been writing on, and experiences I've had in my own life show similarities with Fathers and Sons.

K: Many critics hear echoes of Dostoyevsky.

G: I think Dostoyevskyan overtones in mine and, some South American writing, come from the situation, the society where you are living. In South Africa one often feels only Dostoyevsky could have done justice to the extraordinary lives of blacks.

K: You dissect the evasions of liberalism. But could your technique of distancing be called a liberal strategy?

G: No matter what my convictions might be, it's not my place, nor my purpose, to push them in a novel. I'm wanting to release what others feel. Of course in Berger's Daughter there are convinced Marxists. But there must be a time when you begin to question that system - it's not complete. So I make Rosa see a man die in her lunch hour. As a novelist I could not do them all justice if I did not bring in the great unanswered questions. This I do through Rosa, who fascinates me.

K: And how do you approach blacks?

G: I do not allow, and have no desire to allow, my private prejudices to invade my writing because that leads to some kind of self censorship - every black on your side is on the side of the angels. Your kind of person must be shown as perfect: this is one of the terrible effects of orthodoxy. Even if one is totally against racism, as a writer one must resist tooth and nail those who say you can't show any black who is less than perfect, totally brave and upright. People must be allowed to be human. The writer must be free to deal with our extraordinary Dostoyevskyan variety, the lack of dependability in the human soul.

K: Could you say more about how you do this in your short stories?

G: I sometimes use short stories to explore ideas which I develop in the novels. For example betrayal in 'Oral History', where the black chief reports some young black freedom fighters to the police and instead of their being arrested, sees his whole village bombed. And the girl in my short story 'The Train from Rhodesia' experiences a deep feeling of burning shame when her new husband bargains for a carved lion and pays too little. Well this has happened to me many times in my own life, through the behaviour of people close to me - things they have said or done. It's a kind of drumming bitterness that spreads like a stain. I too have done or said things in such a way that I suddenly feel how corrupted I am by the place that I've been brought up in and the kind of society I've lived in.

K: You insisted that the act of writing fiction is for you inescapably a political act. The novelist must be sooner or later a social critic, with no allegiance to political ideology.

G: The novel I consider a critique of society - it always is even when remote from obvious political or sociological connotation. Even the sloppiest love story has something to do with how that society regards life. But when I began to write in South Africa, that very qualifying phrase 'in South Africa' didn't exist for me, I just began to write, and this is something that no one can explain; one just writes - the way one sings if one has a voice. I did not 'know' then that I was a white writing in a colour bar situation.

K: But your novels demonstrate that you became gradually more aware. July's People is actually set in the future, during a revolution. A white couple are helped to escape by their black servant, July. How did that idea grow?

G: It grew, as always, by things happening around me. And out of a lifelong relationship, as soon as I was conscious at all: the master and servant relationship with blacks is an extraordinary relationship, so intimate, so separate. I'd been brooding on it for years. I'd touched on it in many other stories, such as 'Happy Event'. The kind of relationship I'm exploring is the fruit of maturity, so to speak. When it comes to the style in which it's written I always find only one style is going to be right. Proust put it this way: 'Style is the moment of identity between the writer and the subject.' That's what one looks for. In July's People it seemed that it should be told in this distanced way, unlike Berger's Daughter. That was told in the first person, even when other people are speaking - it's Rosa imagining other people looking at her. But this distanced treatment suits the people here: more or less the average enlightened white people.

But fortunately in South Africa there are some extraordinary black and white people who are prepared to take a Pascalian wager on the fact that there is a way, that there must be a way. It goes beyond polarisation, it cannot happen while the situation is what it is. It can only be <u>after</u> the power structure has changed. But the fact is that if whites want to go on living in South Africa, they have to change. It's not a matter of just letting blacks in - white life is already dead, over. The big question is, given the kind of conditioning we've had for 300 years, is it possible to strike that down and make a common culture with the blacks?

K: T.S. Eliot said that a true writer does not write about experiences he's had, but about experiences he's going to have.

G: Writers are peculiar beings; it's in the nature of their work to know more than they know consciously. It comes from this completely subconscious ability to read signs in human being and doubtless goes deeper than that. Not that I have a particular political perception, far from it. But if one does what writing ought to do - touch fact at a certain point and then invent an alternative life from there, you very often arrive at what is coming from the future.

K: And much of your most recent novel <u>A Sport of Nature</u> is set in a possible future.

G: <u>A Sport of Nature</u> covers over twenty years, even longer than <u>Berger's Daughter</u>, and Rosa (Berger) comes in to tea. I wanted a very different type of heroine, who acts instinctively, sexually.

K: Why were you interested in such a different kind of heroine in an extremely political novel?

G: Because we too often make, we who think we are serious-minded, decisions about who is lightweight and who is not. Over a fairly long life I've observed that we decide who is effective and who isn't and they turn out to be quite different. Heavyweights can be such a disappointment to themselves and others, and perhaps because of bad luck, end up not achieving their goals. I'm interested in the fact that the power behind the throne, like Madame de Pompadour, has always been known as someone's mistress. I was discussing this with friends last night and we tried to think of men in that position. I popped up with Sartre and Simone de Beauvoir, but it wasn't acceptable as they're too equal.

K: So it's the young heroine who makes the political contacts?

G: I feel a fascination with this sort of woman - which will annoy some feminist circles very much, because she climbs her way at the beginning from bed to bed. But she really hasn't much choice. I wasn't trying to create a modern Moll Flanders; but I wanted to show that she's seen so much moral prevarication that the only thing she can trust is her own body. After all she's very young, she's in a precarious position; she goes off with a refugee who's a spy and then he abandons her. She has no money, all she has are her good looks, her nice little body, and some intelligence.

K: But didn't you want to show her developing later on?

G: Yes, from a starting point of a girl stripped, stripped of the middle-class trappings that anger would have given her; stripped of decent middle-of-the-road opinions that pull you in a certain way. In fact it's she and Sasha who make most contacts and are most politically effective.

K: Would you say this is your most optimistic novel so far?

G: Well, many people misread July's People. They said it's what would happen after the Revolution, but it's not, its during. It's civil war - not what life would be like for a white settler in South Africa. Whites must show now, by word and deed, they are prepared to share power with blacks. If you have a common purpose while this struggle is on, as I've seen sometimes with black and white students demonstrating together, then you've got a good chance of a common society afterwards.

K: May I ask what you really think of the white character Pauline? Is there a fatal flaw in her as she does not want to answer all pleas for aid?

G: I have great sympathy for characters like Pauline. She represents some of the confusions of a white person in her situation. Remember that she always has to weigh up every situation as her husband is a civil rights lawyer. That means much more in South Africa; he's defending people in political trials all the time. There's a question of whether his work is not more important than one single gesture she might make of driving one single person to the border. She has constantly to weigh up the value of what she might do and what Joe, her husband, might achieve. She is also feeling guilty because she had just made an excuse and refused to hide someone in her house. In her I reflect the difficulties we all have in South Africa between what your conscience tells you to do, what you fear to do, what is sensible to do. In the end she finds strength when she comes back with her son and throws all caution to the winds.

K: It seems to me that A Sport of Nature is about heroinism. I'd like to challenge your statement that you're not a feminist writer.

G: I suppose that any piece of writing that concerns a woman as central can be interpreted from a feminist point of view. What I meant by feminist novel was something <u>conceived</u> with the idea of proving something about women. I think subconsciously this novel says a lot about what has been done to women and what has formed women's characters. But it was not something planned. Here you have a white woman married to a black man and a black woman married to a white man, and I want to show it's still not an easy thing. In a sense the black woman is still in the old colonial position, her English husband goes off and lives his life, trying not to be changed. She's in no sense a liberated woman. You see it's impossible in South Africa to live your private life and just write about that. You possibly can in Europe, but not in South Africa.

K: Should women writers who are 'serious' enter politics?

G: I don't think there should be any difference between men and women. I'm concerned with the liberation of the individual. I'm not a propagandist. As a writer I'm too selfish to put my talent to that extent to any cause. There will always be an aspect of self-criticism in my work, coming out through my characters. One of them shouts: 'Why should the brave ones among us be forced to be mad?' Political content should be <u>part</u> of the essential truth. If the incident, the story, the book is in a milieu and time when part of the essential truth of that situation is political, then a political element must be there. But you can't judge a work of art as political propaganda. I must take my freedom as a writer to show human beings as they are, warts and all. If you don't, you're becoming a propagandist.

K: Does this dilemma make you feel an affinity with East

European writers?

G: I feel an affinity with Eastern European writers because they suffer from the same thing. No matter how subtly they might write something, what's drawn out of their book will be its pertinence to the political situation out of which they write.

K: Do you long to leave South Africa for holidays in Europe?

G: My daughter lives in France, so I enjoy visiting her. But when I come to France, it's only a holiday, just an interlude. It has deep emotional connections for me because my daughter lives there. However, I'm always disturbed before I leave Africa, I don't quite know why. There's a feeling of leaving behind my responsibilities. At home there are always so many people in trouble. At the back of your mind you remember there's somebody in prison or somebody underground, sleeping in a different place every night.

K: It must be difficult ever to relax?

G: It's difficult to relax in South Africa, because there's a war going on. It's an undeclared war, but it's on and has been for a long time, in many different ways. In that war I know which side I'm on.

K: You showed sympathy with both African sides in A Guest of Honour. That is an impressive study of an emerging African state. Was it Zimbabwe? Your novel is prophetic in its understanding of independence movements.

G: I had no particular country in mind. There are some physical characteristics of Zambia, Zimbabwe, a bit of Botswana and Kenya. The kind of conflict I had read about in many countries. The trade unions were more important in West Africa - but the novelist has <u>imaginary</u> freedom.

K: I'd like to ask you to explain the way minor decisions in your life become major moral decisions in South Africa.

G: I think you can't judge in your life what is a major or minor moral decision. Often when you can't make a major decision at all at some important point in your life, you make it through some kind of divergence from a minor decision. Also you begin to understand crises in your life which you hadn't been able to interpret, when something apparently minor happens.

K: For example?

G: In my novel <u>Berger's Daughter</u>, when Rosa is leaving a political gathering, and is driving back across the veld near Johannesburg, across lots of minor roads - a place where there are lots of tiny roads, not even marked on the map. That is significant of the position of blacks living there.

K: That nobody has bothered to put them on the street map.

G: She gets lost and can't find her way back to the main road. In the course of this she sees a donkey cart coming along. Against the sunlight she sees the silhouette of a man savagely beating the donkey, to get it to go. On the back of the cart is a black family, under rugs. She immediately has the reaction of a well brought-up white person against cruelty to animals. She is full of indignation - then suddenly only sees agony: 'Torture without the torturer'.

With her white authority she could take him to a Police Station. But as she reflects about it, she realises that the cruelty to the donkey arises out of the man's life, which is unimaginable to her: how he suffers, how <u>he</u> is beaten in psychological, and other senses. The violence comes from the violence which is done to him.

K: So this small incident makes her realise where she stands?

G: Yes, that's what I'd describe as my method, in using small incidents like that.

K: Why do you include relatively little physical detail about your characters?

G: I use description sparingly because I prefer to let the reader imagine them, from the way the person speaks, moves or reacts, and a few outstanding clues, if they have some physical characteristic.

K: Does this come from short story writing?

G: Yes, and I still write short stories occasionally. They need significant detail. You're not going to describe a person from head to foot, so maybe the way they move a hand or sit or stoop will create a line from which the reader can build up a picture.

K: All at once?

G: No, that was done in the nineteenth century. Novelists started with when the character was born, described eyes, nose, everything. But I prefer to drop these little sketches or points through the work as it goes along, so that the reader can build up an impression gradually.

K: As in <u>The Conservationist</u>?

G: Yes, there I describe the Boer farmer in quite a lot of

detail because his physical presence is the important thing. It isn't so much what he says, or what anybody else says. He is just in that room, dominating by his physical presence, so that justifies a longer description. At the same time I found his dignity rather funny.

K: How did that idea come to you?

G: When I met a woman in her forties who was <u>afraid</u> to smoke in front of her father. That has become one of my preoccupations: the question of power. So much of life consists of people seeking ways to gain power over others which has interested me very much.

K: Everywhere?

G: Yes, between parents and children. Of course in South Africa, it's connected with political power.

K: Perhaps writers see life in slightly different terms?

G: In my rather long life it seems to me that the two greatest drives, the two most important things in people's lives, are sex and politics.

K: You put it magnificently in <u>A Sport of Nature</u>: 'Skin and hair has mattered more than anything else in the world.'

G: There may be a particular connection between sexuality, sensuality and politics.

K: Uniquely in South Africa?

G: What is apartheid all about? It's about the body, about physical differences, black skin, instead of pink; the whole legal structure is based on the physical, so the body becomes supremely important.

K: And that comes subconsciously into your work too?

G: It's difficult to say whether what goes on in South Africa has strengthened my writing because it seems to me so natural to stay on there. I'm really attached to my country.

K: Do you have to earn that attachment if you're white?

G: You have to show that you support change. In my case that you support a complete revolution, if possible a peaceful one. I use revolution in a broad sense, a complete change of the whole political organisation, from grass roots. It's not enough for a white to say 'Right, I'll be prepared to live under black majority rule,' and sit back, waiting for it to come. You also have to work positively, in whatever way you can, as a human being. I'm not talking about as a writer. Indeed, as far as that's concerned that kind of activity, as a human being working towards progress, takes up time and brings all sorts of distractions which make writing there more difficult.

K: But you find all your topics there?

G: There are wonderful subjects there. There are wonderful mutations in human nature, which you see taking place because people are under such pressure. This is food for every writer.

K: What do you consider the function of a writer in this situation?

G: The function of a writer is to make sense of life. It is such a mystery, it changes all the time, like the light. You see incidents in your life differently. You weave back and forth from past to present. You try to make something coherent out of it. When somebody paints, whether it's abstract, using pure form, or whether it's figurative, you are assembling amorphous things and putting them into an order. It's the same process with writing.

p.d. james

P D JAMES was born in August 1920.

Novels

Cover her Face (1962)
A Mind to Murder (1963)
Unnatural Causes (1967)
Shroud for a Nightingale (1971)
An Unsuitable Job for a Woman (1972)
The Black Tower (1975)
Death of an Expert Witness (1977)
Innocent Blood (1980)
The Skull Beneath the Skin (1982)
A Taste for Death (1986)

Non Fiction

The Maul and the Pear Tree (with
T. A. Critchley, 1971)

K: When did you realise you wanted to be a writer?

J: I think I was born knowing I wanted to be a writer. Some people say why do you write if it's not enjoyable all the time? Psychologically I <u>need</u> to write. I can remember the actual moment when I thought 'My life would be a failure in one important respect if I don't start now.'

K: And how do most of your novels start?

J: Usually with a place, my response to a place. It can be a lonely, sinister stretch of coast, or building, a community. <u>Cover Her Face</u>, my first novel, is rather traditional. Now I consider it somewhat derivative, a country house murder. It's based on a country house in Essex, very like the one I describe.

K: And how far do you use real people?

J: I never consciously use real life people. You are now entitled to ask 'What do you use but your real experience?' I suppose you use yourself. You know what emotions feel, even if you do not experience some of them intensely.

K: Why do you think people enjoy the classical detective story?

J: I suspect it does provide a release from tension. It's a method of exorcising irrational doubts and fears. Whatever happens to the reader in real life, he is not the body on the drawing room floor. However much guilt we may <u>all</u> feel, when the accusing finger of the detective is pointed, we can return a confident 'Not Guilty'.

K: But surely 1930s detective novels were neatly plotted, and reassuring.

J: The 1930s detective novels were particularly reassuring. Perhaps their values were more ordered and settled. There was a more matriarchical, comforting way of life - for the privileged, though far from it for the underprivileged. After the murder the detective comes, order is restored. Eden is restored.

K: I suspect the readership was fairly middle-class. What features attracted readers to those novels?

J: They kept to familiar characters and settings. You know the kind of thing, a small town, local characters, moving on the chess board strictly according to rank and station. They offer the comforting illusion that violence is exceptional, that all policemen are honest, that the English class system has not changed and that murderers aren't gentlemen.

K: Do you think of yourself as more contemporary than that?

J: Oh yes, the books are set in their time and place. They are more realistic, much less optimistic, bleaker. Certainly Eden is not restored, and no life which comes in touch with murder remains unchanged. We may get a solution but not a restoration of order. Nor do we necessarily get justice.

K: Would you say detectives are essentially lonely people?

J: The detective underlines the importance of the individual. Even when he's one of a team, the genre demonstrates the triumph of individual endeavour over evil. Writers must not encumber their detectives with much private life. One way of doing it is to give him a happy marriage and a poor wife who scarcely appears. I cheated, or rather made life easier for myself, by making him a widower. He uses both his job and his grief at his wife's death as an excuse for <u>not</u>

committing himself seriously to human relationships. He has love affairs but I seldom mention them. What he does with consenting females is his business rather than mine.

K: Do you like your detective?

J: I like Dalgliesh very much. A writer can't carry on a character for a series of books without really liking or respecting him. An occupational hazard for us is said to be falling in love with our detective. I think Ngaio Marsh did to a certain extent and Dorothy Sayers certainly did with Sir Peter Wimsey.

K: Do you feel that's happened with you?

J: No, I'm very aware Dalgliesh has a streak of ice in the heart and wouldn't be a good man to fall in love with. Nor do I think I'd like to work for him, but I do respect and like him. You have to, because if you get bored, your poor readers are going to get bored with him too.

K: Why did you create a female private eye in Cordelia Grey?

J: That's interesting. I think I felt 'I have a man, a professional, it's time I had a woman, an amateur, and why not make it a girl?' I wanted to write about Cambridge in high summer. And suddenly the idea came to me of an extraordinary relationship between Cordelia and Benny. A failed Scotland Yard detective and the pathetic agency he's inherited. I don't usually take characters from real life, but there's a lot of my younger daughter in Cordelia in An Unsuitable Job for a Woman.

K: What changes have you noticed towards you, as a woman writer over the last three decades?

J: I don't think I've noticed very much. I suppose I was always conscious of myself as a woman writer, as I'm conscious of myself as a woman. But basically I've always thought of myself as a <u>writer</u>. I was rather optimistic when I began as it never occurred to me there would be any difficulty or prejudice on account of my sex. I remember being horrified in Australia when one of the salesmen said 'It's a pity you have your photo on the back of these books, as a lot of our male readers, who had thought you were a man, might stop reading you.' That sort of prejudice is less today. Of course in this country some of our leading novelists are women. It would be difficult to sustain that sort of sexual prejudice - which seems to be lessening in literature as in other fields.

I may be wrong, but I don't feel it was as strong in literature as in much other employment. If you look back to Jane Austen and the Brontes, we have a tradition of producing good women writers.

K: It's a liberating tradition, isn't it?

J: Yes it certainly is. Though some good women writers have rather a limited range. It's a pity that some who are very good don't turn their attention to larger issues of life. Margaret Drabble tried to do that in <u>The Radiant Way</u>. I like her novels. And many women write beautifully, but they are too often about human relationships in a limited socio-economic group.

K: When you called yourself <u>P.D.</u> James using initials instead of a female first name, was it to free yourself?

J: No, not at all. My memory is that I sometimes wrote 'Phyllis'. Then it occurred to me that 'P.D.' looked short and intriguing. It never occurred to me they'd think me a man. However there was never any doubt in my mind that I'd use my maiden name.

K: Was that to protect your children from questions at school about you?

J: No, I felt the genes in me are James. Though you take your husband's name on marriage, your genes are from your own family. I was only a 'Whyte' by convention. Had there been any doubt in my mind, I'm sure my mother-in-law would have preferred me to use 'James' in case there were anything in the books she didn't like.

K: So being a woman hasn't proved a disadvantage?

J: Not in the thriller, as it's a genre where women have been dominant this century.

K: Have you felt, as many women writers have expressed since the sixties, limitations in our language?

J: We've got the same words as the men; it's up to us to use them effectively and to the best of our ability. I'm not exactly sure what they mean when they say 'free' language. Of course I'm talking about men and women very much in society. I don't feel I want to free language. But I did want to free the classical detective story of some of its constraints, within what is admittedly a popular form. It's a rather dogmatic form, with its own conventions. You need to free the form to be truthful about sexual and other matters.

K: I felt your analysis to be much more contemporary. In fact I found the psychological problems represented strongly.

J: I'm glad. The danger is that you also want to produce a detective story, with <u>clues</u>, and that can become dominant. I hope I never have twisted or distorted psychological truth in order to provide a more exciting story - though it can prove a temptation.

K: How much do you plan - and how much does the writing take over?

J: When writing the process is mysterious. There can come a moment when you have a book plotted in a certain way and suddenly it comes to you 'No, it didn't happen like that.' That happened with the present book. I got halfway, then suddenly realised 'No she would not have done that. It would have been really exciting and make a wonderful ending; but your character would not have behaved like that.' So you realise you're on the wrong path.

K: When you changed from the professional male detective Dalgliesh, to the girl Cordelia, could you look at the stories in different ways?

J: You need clues in a detective story. But of course you have clues in other literature. Look at <u>Emma</u>, which is a wonderful detective story. There are straightforward clues, such as Jane Fairfax going to collect her letters from the Post Office only after her lover has left.

However, with a woman detective you are free from worrying about forced procedures, the constraints of the professional policeman. She can go, and do, and say more or less what she wants. On the other hand, she is not backed up by all the resources of forensic science, fingerprinting, photographers.

K: So a woman is a different kind of detective?

J: To be a detective without all those facilities isn't easy. But it is easier to have a woman as chief character. Especially in smaller ways, Cordelia's agonising about what she'll wear. I often didn't know what Dalgliesh was wearing. Physically I don't see him clearly, just his psychological truth.

K: I admire the way you represent men.

J: Good. But we do not know, and we cannot know, what it <u>feels</u> like to be a man getting up in the morning, shaving, in the way we really know what it's like for a woman.

K: Is that a disadvantage?

J: Not a tremendous disadvantage. It can be a problem for a novelist. It interests me how little it seems to matter, as long as the novel has this power to enter into the thoughts and lives of the opposite sex. I read a lot of Trollope and he's magnificent at the opposite sex.

K: Unlike Dickens.

J: Yes, and Trollope has scenes between women, with no man present, which are astonishingly true to life. I don't know how he does it.

K: So you read more nineteenth than twentieth-century novelists?

J: Yes, but there are some things they couldn't do. For one, the fact that they could not deal openly with sex <u>was</u> a disadvantage for writers. In <u>Middlemarch</u> I do want to <u>know</u> the truth of Dorothea's marriage.

K: How much research do you do?

J: I do a great deal of research before writing. In fact the process of planning, plotting and research takes as long as the actual writing. There's the research that's returning to the actual place, getting the feel of it again, the kind of skies and architecture. Then there's the research about people - or rather getting in touch with your own characters. It sometimes seems to me that I'm not so much creating as getting in touch. As if the whole book exists in a limbo of the imagination and during this preparatory period I'm letting them communicate with me. The process is one of revelation rather than creation.

K: Would you call yourself a religious writer?

J: In some senses I am. Certainly in the books religion does not provide much solace or comfort. It's really there to provide another dimension of life. For me and for many of my characters, there's another dimension which can't be measured - and can't really be subject to the judgement of men. And the detective story is about the judgement of men.

K: In <u>Death of an Expert Witness</u> there is a powerful church presence.

J: It's used twice in a rather powerful way: once when the church is used by two of the characters to make love, and also when a body is found in the porch of a church.

K: Why do churches feature in nearly all your books?

J: Partly I like visiting them, partly because I'm fascinated by the power of contrast they can bring to my novels. In church one has a quiet, sanctified place, a reminder of man's aspirations towards holiness and love. Therefore a church in a crime novel provides a wonderful contrast with this appalling, contaminated murder.

K: Have you tried other genres?

J: Seldom. But <u>Innocent Blood</u> wasn't a detective story.

K: Is that one of your favourites?

J: My favourites are that one and a <u>A Taste for Death</u>. If I could only be left with two, it would be those. The young usually like <u>An Unsuitable Job for a Woman</u> because young Cordelia is in Cambridge, with students.

K: What advice would you give young writers?

J: You must <u>write</u>, not just think you're going to. It doesn't really matter what you tackle first, novel, short story or diary. And you must widen your vocabulary, enjoy words. You must read widely, not in order to copy, but to find your own voice. A student of architecture has to work at other buildings, see what other architects have done and ask why they were so good. It's a matter of going through life with all one's senses alive, to be responsive to experience, to other people.

K: I was struck by your attention to others and to ideas. Do you think one can use a detective novel, so widely read, to express your ideas?

J: You can, but I don't think much of didactic novels. You can introduce anything into detective novels.

K: What do you want to introduce most?

J: The truth about human beings, the truth about the way people somehow manage to cope with their lives. And about the kind of defences we erect against reality. Murder is the ultimate crime, it knocks these defences down. It makes us face what we really are: the conflict between reality and imagining what we are. I deal with men and women in society coping with their own neuroses.

K: Do you have views on female friendship, female solidarity?

J: I think it's very important. Many of us who are women are fond of the company of other women. I certainly am very much, and feel a sense of solidarity. I don't dislike men, nor agree with sections of the women's movement founded on dislike of men. I'm very grateful to many men in my life. But I do appreciate the friendship and support of other women. And I feel lucky to have had daughters.

K: Do you think women can do some things with the novel that men can't?

J: Women are particularly sensitive to the truth of human relationships and often a woman's novel is more clearly rooted in everyday reality, which I very much like. It's astonishing how seldom men tell you what people are wearing or eating - or the problems of everyday life.

K: Which women do that well at the moment?

J: Take Elizabeth Jane Howard, how good she is on food, and the preparation of it; such a tremendous part of life. You seldom get that sense of rootedness in reality in male writing.

K: Who do you imagine your audience to be?

J: Extremely law-abiding, as it's a form of escapism. People who like their escapism to be civilised.

K: Are you read more by women than men?

J: Slightly more, though when I do a signing, I see as many men. Probably slightly more middle-aged than young.

K: Are you read in America as much as Britain?

J: Yes, and when I'm on tour in the States I'm often asked 'Why is it that middle-class, middle-aged English women are so good at murder?' Women are good at a particular <u>kind</u> of detective story; we don't write the hard-boiled private eye kicking down doors. Our books are not as violent - women write malice domestic: 'Stands the church clock still at three/and is there arsenic still for tea?'

K: So you prefer a domestic setting for your novels?

J: They are often set in a village or small town. Auden said he only enjoyed them in a small place, as he liked the contrast between order, peace, normality and sudden crime. We are good at that contract.

K: What other 'female' qualities make a good detective story?

J: Women have an eye for detail, and much of clue-making depends on having an eye for the details of everday living. Possibly women do find the form reassuring simply because it <u>is</u> a way of distancing one's terror of violence. I fear violence a great deal, and I suspect many women do.

K: What ideas can be explored best through your genre?

J: What's interesting to me is to explore some of the organised bridges of law - and religion - that we construct over a great chaos of personal and psychological disorder. One of the attractions of this kind of fiction is that murder blows all this apart. We all create a facade for ourselves, we create a persona, we have our little devices for making life tolerable. Murder, the unique crime, destroys all that. Therefore we see people far more as they really are.

K: Would you say writing is therapeutic?

J: One psychologist said that all creativity is the successful resolution of internal conflict. This is true of myself, and I suspect of many other writers.

K: Your new work as Chairman of the Literature Panel of the Arts Council must be time-consuming. Why did you accept?

J: Because I think I can do it and it is an important job. We only meet once a month, and the Literature Panel meets once a quarter. Being on the Board of the BBC is much more demanding, as I'm a Governor. It's fascinating, and good for a writer to be involved. I had to give up being a magistrate as I couldn't find the time without giving up something. The pressure is created by correspondence from all over the world, the pressure to do extra things, that's tiring. One could have a busy life just dealing with the past.

K: Do you have a different policy of Arts Council than Marghanita Laski?

J: I think there is a case for occasional bursaries, though I don't feel strongly. Encouraging literature and especially helping the young to appreciate literature is probably the most worthwhile. The Arts Council behaved recently as if literature scarcely existed. It's one of our major art-forms and I'm trying to get a fairer allocation of funds. There is lots one can do, though it's not as easy to subsidise literature as to send dance companies round the country. But there is an immense amount that can be done: journals, poetry magazines, which couldn't otherwise exist. Writers in schools, writers on tours.

K: What are you hoping to achieve now?

J: Get this present book finished.

K: It must be nearly three years since <u>A Taste of Death</u>.

J: Exactly, so if it's not next year. I have a minor part to change.

K: Do you carry the characters around wherever you go?

J: Not when I'm speaking to other people, but when I get away, then I move into my characters' world.

K: Do you enjoy that or occasionally want to escape?

J: No, I enjoy it, I like being in the world of the book, as long as I can shut myself away.

K: I understand that, I like most of your characters.

J: I'm glad you say that, as so many people say 'They are all so awful, how can you bear to write about them?' I sometimes answer 'If you're writing a book in which most of the characters are serious suspects for murder, you can't expect them to be members of the Parochial Church Council and little angels of light.'

K: What do you think of some feminism today?

J: I am a feminist in that I like my own sex. In history we have not been treated fairly by the other sex. Our advancement depends on economic advancement, to give women a better chance in life, the ability to earn their own living. If you are totally dependent on men economically you are not going to have real freedom. But I'm not a hater of men. I don't agree with the view that they are all potential rapists or child molesters. We are all potential murderers. Of course if you've had bad experiences at the hands of men, that view is understandable. But for the rest of us it's self-defeating.

K: So you find the extreme edges of feminism

unattractive?

J: Perhaps women today aren't wiling enough to accept
that we have to make choices. Often when children
are young we have the choice of looking after them or
paying someone else. I think the happiest children
are the ones whose mother <u>did</u> enjoy looking after
them.

K: Did looking after them prevent your starting to write?

J: I was late in starting, as I felt rather mixed up. I was
already in my thirties when I wrote my first novel.

K: But surely you'd written before then?

J: Just bits and pieces. I was very lucky with my first
novel, it was accepted by the first publisher it was sent
to - the first book I ever completed. My husband came
home sick from the war, so I had to get a safe job as I
had him and two daughters to support. That's why
I've been a working wife all my life.

K: Very demanding.

J: I don't think I could do it now - though in a way I'm still
doing it, with all my extra jobs such as Chairman of
the Society of Authors till last year and I'm still on its
Council.

K: Do you have to sacrifice a great deal of life outside
work?

J: Yes, but I'm not a party-goer. I loathe noisy crowded
rooms, and clutching warm white wine. What I love
is seeing my friends and small dinner parties.

K: Is there anything you regret?

J: No, I've been a fortunate woman. There is only one thing I regret: I'd like to have gone to university. I left school at sixteen. But I was at a good old-fashioned grammar, and was lucky there. I'd like to have written a good play, to try a different type of literature. In fact I did write a short play, which had a three-week run, but it was too literary.

K: Would you prefer the theatre because it means working with other people, discussing your writing?

J: No, I love working on my own. And when a book is published, I travel to promote it. I've been to Australia and from the east to the west coast of the United States. Exhausting, but very interesting for me as a person and as a novelist.

iris

murdoch

IRIS MURDOCH was born in Dublin in July 1919.

Novels	Under the Net (1954)
	The Flight from the Enchanter (1955)
	The Sandcastle (1957)
	The Bell (1958)
	A Severed Head (1961)
	An Unofficial Rose (1962)
	The Unicorn (1963)
	The Italian Girl (1964)
	The Red and the Green (1965)
	The Time of the Angels (1966)
	The Nice and the Good (1968)
	Bruno's Dream (1969)
	A Fairly Honourable Defeat (1970)
	An Accidental Man (1971)
	The Black Prince (1973)
	The Sacred and Profane Love Machine (1974)
	A Word Child (1975)
	Henry and Cato (1976)
	The Sea, the Sea (1978)
	Nuns and Soldiers (1980)
	The Philosopher's Pupil (1983)
	The Good Apprentice (1985)
	The Book and the Brotherhood (1987)
Plays	The Severed Head (1964)
	The Italian Girl (1969)
	The Servants and the Snow (1973)
	The Three Arrows (1973)
Poetry	A Year of Birds (1978)
Non Fiction	Sartre: Romantic Rationalist (1953)
	The Sovereignty of Good (essays, 1970)
	The Fire and the Sun: Why Plato Banished the Artists (1977)

G: I know you don't like the word 'intuition' when allied to the creative process in novel-writing as an attempt to describe what it is that produces the world of imagination, but you did use the word 'subconscious' recently in saying something about that process, that the means by which a writer creates his art may have something to do with the 'subconscious'. I wonder if you could amplify that?

M: I mean it in the Freudian, or quasi-Freudian, sense simply. It is not necessary to go into the scientific question of how exactly the word should be understood in order to decide whether or not such a thing exists. One is aware of a large dark area of one's mind from which all sorts of ideas and images emerge, and certainly in the invention of stories this great abyss can provide unexpected material. There is a well-tried maxim about 'sleeping on it', when you ask yourself a question at night and find the answer there in the morning. At any rate when one is tired after trying hard to solve some problem, the answer may come unexpectedly, as if hidden forces had been working on it. I think any artist knows this well, that extra-ordinary imagery and very strange ideas can appear unexpectedly. Think of dreams; here it seems that an extraordinary inventive process is going on of which one knows very little.

G: I wanted to ask you if you have a switch-on, switch-off sensibility which operates when you sit down to write a novel, but doesn't necessarily need to operate when you write a letter to a friend?

M: I suspect that most writers, when writing anything, find that whatever it is is permanently switched on. If I write to my bank manager I can't write an ordinary letter to him (I don't know what he thinks about it), but the process of writing is so much a part of the whole being of the person that one would write letters as a writer does, obviously not with any kind of self-consciousness but just because the machinery is there, and one is using it.

G: You have written novels since 1953, when <u>Under the Net</u> came out, a considerable number. Are you ever accused of being too prolific?

M: I think it depends on how much energy and imagination one has. I am certainly surprised, looking back, at a time when I was doing a full- time job - because I did a full-time teaching job until 1963 or 1964 - that I still managed to do this work, which I could only manage, of course, in the vacations. Any artist has the problem of how fast he is going to work, and when he is to decide when something is finished. I am very meticulous about what I do: I always write two drafts, that is the novel is always written all the way through twice, and many parts are written ten times. The period of primary invention is the hardest and most important time.

Yes, it seems to have come fast, but speaking for myself I don't think it has come too fast.

G: Your reference to teaching brings me to the next point, the fact that you are a teacher as well as a writer, and also a critic of literature. Does the one in any way impede the other? The fact that half of you has to stand aside objectively and think of literature in a critical sense - does this interfere with the free, creative side of you, or do they mutually interact?

M: I am not a critic, and I don't write much about literature. I know a certain amount about English literature, and I am interested in other languages too, so I have various literary interests; but I'm not a professional critic, and I think there is a large difference between somebody who has ideas and someone who is an expert and I am not an expert. As far as philosophy is concerned, there is a conflict in terms of time. Philosophy is very difficult and demands one's whole attention too, so that one is in difficulties here. I continue to do philosophy, although I'm not teaching it now, but I occasionally give lectures. I would like to write more philosophy. There is always a conflict and involves one in decisions about how one is going to spend one's time.

The activities are totally different. I'm not a philosophical novelist, and I don't want the philosophy to get into the novels since it's a different game, a different way of thinking and a different way of writing.

G: You have written a book with the title The Sovereignty of Good, a refulgent title with a Richard Baxter feel about it, almost like the work of a great Puritan divine, and you constantly stress that the condition of reality is an unselfed, and 'unselving' love. This suggests a religious quality in yourself, although you would question this, I am sure. But I wonder if there is a sense of the religious within your work at its deepest levels, or is it that art is more important to your expression than the explicit experience of religion?

M: I wouldn't question your earlier phrase about the religious aspect. I grew up as a Christian. I don't believe the literalistic Christian dogmas any more. But I feel very close to Christianity and to the Christian religion; and I'm interested in religion, too, which is a slighty different point; I am very interested in Buddhism, for instance.

Yes, there is a religious aspect, and this is something which has increased, perhaps, and about which I have grown more confident - though perhaps not wholly confident. Certainly it is something which has appeared more over my horizon.

G: The audience for this tape will include librarians, students or their teachers, and they will be interested to know how you set about organising your sources of information when you sit down to write a novel. Whatever the subject, it requires data, facts about characters, situation or setting. Do you have a systematic way of garnering the information you may need about people, habits, even trivial details?

M: I often use libraries. I am lucky enough to live in Oxford and I do use the Bodleian if necessary; for instance for the Irish novel, <u>The Red and the Green</u>, a historical novel about the Irish rebellion I spent a considerable amount of time in the Bodleian and this was very rewarding. Of course that is a unique library, there was everything there, all kinds of contemporary pamphlets which I needed to look at, and it was a marvellous experience just to have all this material turning up. One was able to do a good deal of quite minute research easily and reasonably fast, and I have used it for other purposes too. One should try to get things right.

G: How do you feel about your audience? You have given a talk, with your husband John Bayley, on the 'Theory and Practice of Novels', and the question of the 'sharing' of a work with an unseen audience was part of this. Do you feel conscious of your audience at all? Is this necessary or even possible for a novelist?

M: I don't feel conscious of an audience, no. I think the sharing process happens at a deep level. It is an interesting and important question, the matter of what, when you are explaining something - and a novel is a great piece of explanation - you take for granted, and what you feel you have to tell. But I think much of this takes place instinctively; it involves the decisions that you make about what sort of morality you take for granted and what you feel has got to be invented or put on the table by you, and also of course what sort of sheer factual information you assume in your audience. Otherwise I don't feel particularly conscious of an audience, though I'm glad there is an audience; it makes a difference to any artist whether he feels he is showing his work or not: writers in some countries just have to put the stuff away since they know they cannot publish it. Any writer is happier if his material is being offered to an audience, but who the audience consists of, how many there are, or how educated I don't think bothers me.

G: What is the difference between a best seller and a serious writer? Is it possible to define this?

M: Some serious writers are best sellers. I think that's hard to define, and one would have to take individual works and look at them. I think most writers are serious, or at any rate partly serious if they are producing stuff - which though it sounds like a tautology - has some pretensions to seriousness. Obviously there might be pornographic writers or certain kinds of thriller writers who have no object except to produce stuff which will sell; but writing is such a personal business that people invest their thoughts and feelings in what they write, even if they are writing at a popular level.

G: But when a Harold Robbins produces a number of best sellers, there is somehow a suggestion of the meretricious, that he is calculating his effects and the necessary ingredients in a novel to reach a larger number of readers. Or is this a cynical assessment?

M: I haven't read anything by him, and I think there are people who do this in a cynical way, but I find it hard to imagine that even if one started off as a cynic one wouldn't be converted by one's own work.

G: A question which has troubled me for some time is this: is it possible for the novelist to invent the mimic world that he constructs as a paradigm of the world we live in any longer? Because today the novelist is in competition with so many other media of fact, and the conveyance of experience - films, television, the documentary. Is the old figure of the omniscient novelist able to speak in the same way when he can't even be a specialist, there is such a multiplicity of subjects now, requiring specialisation on the one hand, and on the other the journalists? Is the novelist being driven into himself and becoming a more subjective person because of this?

M: I shouldn't think because of this, exactly. I think he is probably being driven into himself and perhaps becoming more subjective, but I doubt that the proliferation of television and journalistic information really affects the novelist very much because after all he is dealing with the great central subjects of human life. Some novelists set up as documentary people themselves, and might want to write a novel about the Olympic Games which would be a kind of reportage and it need not necessarily be a bad novel either, but the ordinary novelist is dealing with the same old subjects, with love and marriage, and good and evil, and struggling through life, and facing death, and what kind of particular setting he gives to his novel is no more problematic than it was.

I think there may be very general reasons why novelists are now less good. It is indeed a fact that compared with the nineteenth-century giants, contemporary novelists are less good, and quite apart from a sheer lack of talent, this may be to do with a less clear, less confident, concept of the individual's relation to his society. This would need a lot of explanation. I haven't in fact got any very clear notion of why this change has taken place.

I doubt that the novelist is much bothered by the media, because he is an egoist and lives in his own world and believes in his own mode of operation, and feels he is separate from all that world of ephemera. It wouldn't for a second occur to me that I was competing with anything except myself and a conception of some of the great people in the past, and even then the word 'competition' wouldn't be appropriate.

G: What would you say you were setting out to achieve by teaching young people philosophy? What is the ultimate value of that particular scheme of education, a degree in philosophy?

M: At Oxford, philosophy comes in a package, either with politics, economics and some history, or in the classical degree which I did myself, 'Greats', which includes Greek and Latin language and literature, and Ancient History. I think Greats is a very good degree, a marvellous education because it gives you in its four-year course a tremendous vision of the classical world and of the languages, which are useful also in a scholarly sense, and the world of Ancient History, a wonderful world I feel at home in, a world I identify with, both the Greek and Roman classical scene; then philosophy, which begins with Plato and Aristotle and goes on to the present day.

I think philosophy is extremely good training for anyone who wants to do anything. Although that is an idea which people may speak scornfully of now, I think it does teach one to <u>think</u>, it teaches judgement insofar as it can be taught, it gives a confidence in dealing with the conceptual problems wherever they arise, and of course they arise everywhere. For instance, I was, because of the War, directed immediately after my degree into the Civil Service, and I found that in doing that completely different sort of work the philosophical training did help. It does clarify the mind, quite apart from the innate interest of a subject in which one is dealing with the greatest minds of the past struggling with the greatest problems in human life. I was very touched to get a letter from an Indian girl who had been a pupil of mine and was now back in India and struggling with great difficulties since she was involved in politics, and constantly in debate and argument, and she said 'I feel like a giant here, because I can think much more clearly than most of my opponents.' She attributed this to having studied philosophy.

G: Does it help people to have a deeper moral sense, or not necessarily? Is it a subject laid out, like botany, and no more involving of the whole psyche?

M: I think many people do philosophy without having any idea of its connecting with religion or, in a deep sense, with morality. This is partly a matter of temperament, and it is hard to say what it is in people that makes them want to reflect about religion or morals. The reasons for this go deep into each individual's life. I believe many people are inspired by this aspect of philosophy - I think I was, perhaps not so much when I was an undergraduate, but later on. Contact with great moralists, such as Kant or Plato, can stir and clarify one's imagination and reflection. One can be taught to <u>think</u> about these matters. The great metaphysicians offer us explanatory pictures of human existence.

G: A philosopher could use the word 'love' without embarrassment?

M: That is an interesting question. I think many modern

philosophers would feel they should avoid terminology of that sort; they would feel it could not be translated into the kind of philosophical terms they are using. It is a concept which is deliberately excluded by those who create certain types of philosophical terminology, it would suggest to them a religious approach, or they would find it was a muddled idea which they couldn't use.

But after all love holds a central position in human life, and Plato, who founded western philosophy, placed it in his concept of Eros. Platonism passed into Christian theology. Philosophers should turn to these matters. I also believe that it is time for philosophy and theology to attend to each other.

G: Which brings me to two words that I have seen you use in your books and perhaps I could ask you briefly about them. Somewhere you wrote that your theme is 'transient mortal creatures subject to necessity and chance'. What do you mean by 'necessity' and what do you mean by 'contingency'?

M: In a sense the two concepts are the same, for what looks like chance in one context is necessity in another. I simply mean the way in which human life so relentlessly forces people into patterns which they have only half chosen, or not chosen. If one thinks of any human life, it is full of irrevocable decisions, paths which diverge, and you are a totally different person if you choose one path, from the one you would have been if you had chosen the other path. And there are painful kinds of necessity involved in most people's lives: they have to do a job they don't want to do, they have to live in a place they don't want to live in. Everything to do with family life is full of necessity.

Certain kinds of philosophy - Existentialism, for instance, a philosophy with which I disagree - and certain quasi-philosophical attitudes suggest that human life is full of choices and that in reality one is totally free. I think this is an illusion. Free will operates within a small area. One is surrounded by a causality which one only partially understands; in fact one can understand very little about one's situation, and this is what it's like to be human. Causality may meet you in the guise of a choice that is forced upon you, where you do at least see what is happening; or else in the form of an encounter with a motor car in the middle of the road. Chance in that awful sense is always with us.

G: Is that what Camus was trying to struggle with in L'etranger [The Outsider] when Meursault is presented to us as someone who appears to be free of the normal bourgeois choices that bother us all day long? Would you say that novel was successful in that respect?

M: It is a memorable novel. I'm not sure about what you say, it is complicated by the personality of the chap, Camus wants to present him as a doomed man, doomed by a sort of mad liberation which has come upon him. I think well of the novel, but I think there is something murky in the conceiving of it, which is part of its force. It seems to me that there is a kind of demonic element involved which isn't anything to do with thoughts about freedom, but something in Camus' mind, some deep thing of his own. Meursault looks to me like a man with an obsession; and obsessions obstruct liberty.

G: When you feel like saying 'I'm deeply moved by a novel', what exactly, as far as one can be exact about this, would this mean to you? What qualities in it would have that affect upon you?

M: There are good novels of so many different kinds, that

is what is so marvellous about the novel, and one is moved in many different ways. I think it is the Shakespearean quality in great novels that moves one - that is an idea I keep coming back to - when a novelist can present a human drama and character in a significant way and at the same time with great art, often making it very funny, too; the great novel is always funny, in fact I think the novel is essentially a comic form, (tragedy is for the theatre) not meaning by that full of jokes, but that it is about the absurd detail of human life, the way in which one cannot fully understand what is happening. Life is muddle and jumble and ends inconclusively, and when this is presented with great comic art the sorrows of human life can be truthfully conveyed; one is moved by the spectacle, and feels that something truthful has been told in a magical way. In Shakespeare you have a dramatic story wherein something true and often intellectually very profound is contained, completely transmuted into poetry and magic. This is what I think a great novel does too.

G: You said you thought Shakespeare was the top novelist.

M: Yes, I think so. Of course he is not a novelist, but he does what novelists ought to be trying to do, and he has the advantage of the magic of poetry, and this makes the whole thing different in a way; yet I think the particular free quality in Shakespeare, the way in which he produces great free characters and yet relates them together and has a pattern which is not an obsessive pattern but a beautiful pattern, a magical pattern in a non-obsessive free sense - this is what one must attempt to do.

G: I wonder if we can conclude with one or two questions about writing, for example: what sort of relations have you had with publishers? Have they been agreeable, are they easy people to deal with, or are they demanding?

M: I've been lucky. I happened immediately upon two publishers, one English, one American with whom I've had perfect relations, in fact they are my friends. I think writers do often have difficulties, but it's a matter of luck who you land up with. There can be feuds - I know some who are involved in feuds with their publishers, and this is painful and I'm glad that I am not.

G: Did your first manuscript travel very far before it was accepted - your first novel, <u>Under the Net</u>?

M: That wasn't by any means the first novel I wrote. I wrote several novels, or parts of novels, before that, which were very bad, and which I just put away, and one I tried on a publisher who rightly turned it down, and I put that away and tried again. When <u>Under the Net</u> came along I did have a certain confidence in that, and the first publisher I offered it to accepted it.

G: How do you feel about Creative Fellowships in Writing, and Arts Council grants, the kind of encouragement one sees on all sides nowadays - though presumably writers say insufficiently. Is it relevant to what a writer can do, or what he's about?

M: I think a writer would be very unwise to imagine that he can live by writing, and I think that particularly for a young writer it's probably better if he does another job anyway rather than regarding himself as a dedicated isolated figure who somehow has a right to live alone and write. This sounds hard, because doing a full-time job and trying to write at the same time is painful and also of course may be wasteful of a person's talent - it is a difficult point. I would think that writers would be well advised to have an ordinary job, particularly as living on grants is dicey, since there's very little money available; I would regard that as an emergency relief operation for artists. There are artists, such as sculptors, who need expensive material, and a grant would enable them to do a big work which they couldn't otherwise do. Writers don't in that sense need material, they need time. I can think of somebody who is a very talented novelist, now trying to complete a work but, with three children, she is in all sorts of difficulties from which she could be relieved by some money; even if this helped her for a year it would be a great benefit. I think the Arts Council tries to find out situations of that sort and give emergency relief, and this is an important function.

G: And Public Lending Right?

M: Yes. I think that is very important, especially for writers who are not writing, but whose books are continually being read.

michele

roberts

MICHELE ROBERTS was born in 1949.

Novels	A Piece of the Night (1978) The Visitation (1983) The Wild Girl (1984) The Book of Mrs Noah (1987) Seven Deadly Sins (1988)
Poetry	Touch Papers (1982) The Mirror of the Mother (1986)
Short Stories	Tales I Tell My Mother (ed. Zoe Fairbairns 1978) More Tales I Tell My Mother (ed. Zoe Fairbairns 1987)
Essays in	Walking on the Water (Virago, 1984) Gender and Writing (Pandora, 1984) Fathers: Reflections by Daughters (Virago, 1984)

K: When did you begin writing?

R: Many times: when I was five, when I was eight, and when I was sixteen I began seriously. I don't know why, but I've always loved language, and I was the storyteller amongst us children. My wonderful grandmother used to tell stories and make up epics and long rhyming rude stories about, for example, pissing in chamber pots, which we children loved. And I told stories to my brothers and sisters every night. Then when I was about eight I discovered I could write neat rhyming poems. I was a prig, sucking up to my teachers, so I produced neat pretty little things. They were revolting as poetry, but pleasurable: they made me seem a good little girl. I kept writing failed novels and failed poems. Then at sixteen I was asked to dance by a boy I'd loved for two years. I was suddenly so overcome by sexual shame that I ran all the way home and started to pour out my adolescent sexual anguish in a poem. It was about Adam and Eve and passion. I realised that if you feel strongly, involving all of you, you have to write, to sort it out.

K: Were your poems like ones you'd read at school?

R: No, they weren't like anything I'd read at school, which was written by men and didn't seem real to me, about anything near to me.

K: Do you put much of yourself in your writing?

R: I don't see how you can't. The impulse to write is so personal, it comes from inside you, whether you write thrillers or garden books. If it's something that matters to me, issues that are important to me, then in that sense I'm in the book. I don't think I'm there as a character any more, though in my first two novels I certainly was. The heroines of those first two novels are to some extent me. I was brought up to think good

novels should exclude 'me'. I was taught good writing
was to leave yourself out. Ironically, the more I tried
to get away from putting myself in books, the more I
was there anyway. Yet the more I allowed myself to
be <u>in</u> the books, the more freedom and power I felt as
a writer to create characters who are bits of me or not
me or bits of me I haven't yet found out about at all.

K: So there's a great deal you can't fully account for in the
process. Do you consider that you are writing what a
lot of women are feeling?

R: Yes, because I don't have a sense of the writer as a
completely separate ego who has clear lines round
herself and is totally original. You have to let go of a
personal self and tune into what's going on, what
other women are thinking - and men to a certain
extent. That's probably why we see certain images
cropping up at the same time. For example,
independently, two of my friends have started writing
books about Arks and archetypes, at the same time as
I was writing <u>Mrs Noah</u>; we were tuning in to the
image of the ark as relevant to our time.

K: Do you write mainly to communicate or is it a very
private experience?

R: A book is an ambitious project for me, and it's about
wanting to be read. Even if I seldom meet my readers,
it's important to me that the reader exists and is
giving <u>back</u> to me by reading. That process is about
two people: the book exists by being read. However
when I'm writing, I'm trying to translate my material
and my symbols, so it feels private while I'm doing it.
But you've got to imagine the reader even then,
otherwise you can't translate into a language that's
accessible - even when it's tricksy or poetic. For me
writing is a way of trying to connect the outside world
and the inside world. The reader is essential. However

if you have too clear an idea of who your audience is, you begin to censor; though I need to feel a reader out there, I don't want to feel I ought to please her too much and start altering things.

K: Is there an ideal reader?

R: My grandmother. She was fantastically supportive of my writing and tolerant of me being the 'bad' girl of the family. She was very forgiving and used to say 'Go on girl, you storyteller, you fibber'. And she would read my novels, at her age. She read my first, about a Lesbian love affair, and kept saying, 'Miche, I don't quite get it, but if I read it enough I know I will.' I was so touched. She was my ideal listener. I still think of her each time I begin a new book.

K: What were reactions to that first novel of yours about Lesbian love?

R: It's also about women's friendship, my childhood in France (the next was about my childhood in England) and about trying to love women and all the difficulties of that. I thought the reviews wonderful. Reactions were mixed, but it was widely reviewed, which helped. Some men wrote that it was about 'shrieking Lesbian banshees'. It was published in 1976, so it was amongst the first of this new wave of feminist novels on women's love.

K: How did readers react to your third book, on Mary Magdalene, The Wild Girl? When I read it I thought you'd have some Christians complaining.

R: Quite a few wrote to me upset that I'd connected the divinity of Jesus with sexuality. Someone sent my book to the Attorney General, without having read it. That alerted a few believers, who then went out and bought it, and tried to get me prosecuted for blasphemy.

I got letters saying 'You'll burn in Hell and I'm very glad.' What surprised me was the amount of homicidal rage, people wanting my death. I answered them all and with some kept up a correspondence so that we ended respecting each other's position. Three or four letters were really nasty, but others were interested and the Movement for the Ordination of Women invited me to come and speak, which was touching.

K: Some people still seem disturbed by talk of women's sexuality.

R: The Church has never been comfortable with our bodies, I think it's as basic as that. It even used to 'church' women after childbirth, to 'cleanse' them. You could only hint at what you felt about your body within the Church when I was a girl. That's very disappointing if you're somebody who is interested in words. I wanted to imagine a woman who was religious and sexually active and unmarried: the Church has no woman saints who were sexually active and involved with spirituality.

K: You would have thought many people would find that relevant.

R: Well it's important for lots of women who are believers. Have you read The Color Purple by Alice Walker? I wept buckets at the end where Shug is talking about God and she says God's into colours and food and sex. It's the first time I'd read something like that in a novel.

K: The Bible contains fairly explicit sexual imagery in The Song of Solomon.

R: That's the part I'll always go back to with enormous pleasure. It's a wonderful love song, but I was brought up to read it as an image of Christ's love for the church in spite of the erotic language.

K: In Hebrew there are about eight words for different types of love.

R: That's part of the richness of the Bible. If you're in a culture which has it as the holy book then it's a treasure house you can keep going back to. When you reread the stories, look at them as literature, it's so alive.

K: And different for each one of us?

R: Yes, each of us will even make up a different story about this room. And when we read novels, we may each have a different interpretation which we'll hold to passionately. It's productive to read the Bible that way.

K: Are you looking at the stories partly to see how they shape us?

R: To some extent the stories we read <u>do</u> shape us. Of course it's such a complex question, the extent to which we are shaped by a culture, and how far we do the shaping. I feel it's a matter of push and pull.

K: What do you think of the stories we read to children?

R: If they can help a child not to judge in terms of goodies and baddies, but to see there's 'evil' in himself as well as outside, that's good. It's such a tough topic to grapple with, if we can help people see the evil in themselves, which is hinted at in the Grimms' stories, then they'll be encouraged, perhaps, to stop saying, 'I'm good and that politician is all bad.'

K: Why should so many children's stories be frightening do you think?

R: Folktales can terrify. The imaginative world of the child contains frightening things, like hate for parents; fairytales can help a child who, for example, can't deal with her hate for her mother alongside her love for her. So a story with a wicked stepmother can help in a simple split way, at that level of development.

K: Are you interested in them as a feminist?

R: In the way one can rewrite these tales to give girls a more central role, as my friend Sara Maitland does. Boys traditionally have quests and kill giants and marry princesses and have their roles confirmed. Too often. But these old stories can be rewritten in too moral a way, without contacting that deep level of symbol. I still find the image of Rapunzel shut up in the tower riveting. I still dream in that way, which can be frightening. Of course if you only get a diet of old fashioned stories with little conflict of gender roles, then you encourage people to think this is how the world is shaped. I'm interested in stories which offer some ambiguity, where the seventh son is the weakling, or where the girl can dress up and become something else. To a great extent stories shape our imaginations, we are talking about the whole role of a culture.

K: How far do you feel limited by language? Are you struggling with words?

R: You are pushing towards a place in language where meaning dissolves, where craziness is going on, where there is extreme poetry without the logic of the rational mind. You have to make a decision about where to stop. I sometimes feel I haven't gone far enough. When you give up rational language you start to feel somewhat crazy as you've gone into a place where logic no longer exists. In the unconscious the words are dancing about like bumble bees. My room can be full of bumble bees, quite chaotic. I've got to let that happen, like an experience of rebirth. You must let out the bumble bees, in order to get anything good, yet it's a scaring process, and I sometimes feel like hiding under my duvet.

K: Is it the same scaring process in all your books?

R: I experimented with different kinds of prose and poetry in my first two novels. They gave me this bumble bee experience, partly because they were about such deep levels of feeling and being. I had to abandon my adult self to get the novels together.

K: And in <u>Wild Girls</u>?

R: I was using a completely different sort of language, inherited; the inherited language of the Bible. The gospel form is less crazy. It is an interesting form, a narrative going more or less from A to Z, and for the first time I used the past tense. When you write narrative you have problems in deciding which sentence comes after which. In the first two novels I was mixing everything up, so I could play with times, even in the sequence of sentences. Narrative is an even more demanding form.

K: Is it difficult to describe what is going on?

R: Yes, words are physical to me, they almost destroy you, tossing you about, and then you start to play with them and toss <u>them</u> about. Carter I admire as she's pushing quite far, to a remote boundary.

K: She feels an affinity with Third World writers, as they have also been marginalised. Have you experienced that, not finding the words you want?

R: Yes, that's why I ended up using very poetic prose for

my novels. It seemed necessary, in order to be able to write about what really goes on between a mother and her daughter and then connect that with history, and the body and the Church. Layers of meaning, which poetry allows, are very important for me. You need images to write about everything at once.

K: You are one of the few women I've met who can write about violence.

R: I was shocked myself, as I don't think of myself as a really violent person, though I can get very angry. But if some of the people in my stories are capable of violence, then I knew I had to be too. There's one episode in Mrs Noah that's about a sado-masochistic affair which I found deeply disturbing to write. But I knew what it was about. I also described a woman battering a baby, to acknowledge we're all human, all capable of these things. You have to face 'evil' inside yourself which is upsetting but necessary. I don't want to split people into good and bad.

K: As in our unconscious?

R: Yes, the Ark is the unconscious in a way, in The Book of Mrs Noah. My narrator wants to walk on the top deck where everything is good and nice; but she discovers there's a lot of chaos underneath. At the end there's a great whirling teaparty in the Ark - how I see my unconscious, full of violence and nasty things as well as stories and my family.

K: Do you feel you are writing poetry?

R: Not quite. I'm saying violent and nasty bits are connected to good, lovely things. That's a much tougher message than saying 'Look, here's evil, and it's simply delicious and wicked'. I want to connect the parts of ourselves that are childish and atavistic with the parts that have to make moral decisions. It's about the difference between fact in life and fact in the imagination. The more we try imaginatively to contain a knowledge of all these horrors, the more we are equipped to fight against them. The less we think about them and imagine them the more likely we are to be overwhelmed by them. I'm sure children can be driven by total despair, thinking they are uniquely awful, devils. The more we imagine, and understand, and talk to each other, the more we can create a climate where we don't have to <u>do</u> the thing.

K: You're idealistic, though it accords with much writing on violence in the twentieth century, for example on the psychology of fascism.

R: The psychology of how fascism gripped the German people is fascinating. Of course there were strong economic and political reasons for fascism; but on a deeper level, it's as if too many people wanted a strong parent telling them what to do. We've got these archetypes in us and the more conscious we are of them, the less likely we are to be overwhelmed by them.

K: How do you rate yourself as a writer? Can you step outside yourself and judge?

R: When you're writing a book you are also using that part of the mind which edits and compares and qualifies a great deal, otherwise you'd never go through draft after draft to get it as good as you can. I believe in pushing myself as much as I can - I suppose I think I've improved.

K: What's your reaction to reviews?

R: Total terror. I still feel total terror, but I've been very lucky, I've had a lot of positive feedback from readers.

And of course I know that my books sell. My first book stuck out, one of the first feminist novels of the generation. A woman on the <u>Sunday Times</u> accused me of witchcraft, of writing about horrors; Lesbians devouring each other and their mothers. She described me as one of 'these mad wild women and lefties who want to destroy Western civilisation'. Whereas others commented 'She writes quite well this girl, a little like Colette.' You couldn't have asked for a richer range.

K: What keeps you writing when things go wrong?

R: You want to improve as you see the flaws in what you've done. If you wrote a perfect book you might not want to continue.

K: Tell me more about your novel <u>The Book of Mrs Noah</u> which was published in 1987. I found the writing incredibly exciting, the images were so unusual - and relevant to women.

R: The first three novels had been about women on quests. This one is about relative failures. I'd been brought up to think that only men write, so I wanted to explore the conflicts for me in images of women as creators and artists. There's a certain amount about my private life in the background, my own specific problems. I was then in Italy, working in libraries, called archives in Italian. The idea of the ark came to suggest to me both a woman's body and a storehouse for old books which I love. I've worked as librarian and love dusty old rooms full of books. Ideas around arks, archives, the pregnant body, came together.

K: It's a religious image also, God flooding a sinful world.

R: Yes. I kept having dreams about the world emptying, destroyed - as I did when writing <u>The Wild Girl</u>. I dreamed of the women at Greenham Common in their

Peace Camp. After rewriting the New Testament in
<u>Wild Girl</u>, I started on the Old Testament here.

K: Why do you find religion such a rich source?

R: Well, I was brought up as a Catholic. Religion is
closely linked to myth, and myth-making fascinates
me. Myth and religion describe our lives in deeply
symbolic ways - and help us to imagine what happens
in death.

K: But surely you are more interested in the potential of
myths here?

R: I became interested in Greek myths about women like
Persephone, who rises every spring. Greek mythology
allows strong women, female friendship; images of
mothers and daughters. The medieval Christian
plays make fun of Mrs Noah. I wanted to look at the
story from her point of view.

K: But she's not as important as your five Sybils, whom
I enjoyed.

R: They are five writers, all with writer's block; they
come on board the Ark for refuge, a breathing space.
I wanted restorative images, in fact I need images to
counteract cultural images of the writer being male,
which go so deep into the unconscious. I had thought
of excluding all males, but God insisted on coming in
as 'the gaffer'. He has writer's block too, because after
writing the Bible, it's difficult to see what more he
could write.

K: But surely it's about the <u>process</u> of writing?

R: Yes, about when the process works, and when it
doesn't. And women writing together - or rather living
together and planning to write.

K: I thought the section on the writers' collective extremely amusing. Of course you have collaborated three times now with other women haven't you?

R: We wrote <u>Tales I Tell my Mother</u> in a sort of collective, meeting regularly and discussing: Sara Maitland, Zoe Fairbairns, Valerie Miner and Michelene Wandor. We read out our stories to each other and criticised each other's work and decided who should write which linking essay, but the writing as such wasn't collective.

K: So much as collaborative?

R: Yes, and such a good experience that we continued eight years later with <u>More Tales I tell my Mother</u> also published by Journeyman Press, which was really supportive.

K: What are you writing at the moment?

R: My present novel puzzles over whether there is a life after death. Can we communicate telepathically through history? I'm looking at whether women from the past communicate with us through their <u>writing</u>, or whether there is <u>haunting</u>, a simple matter of ghosts.

K: Do you believe in ghosts?

R: As a writer, yes; as a human being, I believe in the astonishingly rich powers of the human imagination. One of my women characters is a medium, who was involved in a nineteenth-century <u>cause célèbre</u>. It's a topic I researched before writing, as I think one must keep an open mind. Occasionally I feel psychic. I remember once in Italy feeling acute stomach pains, and having to go to bed; then later that evening my brother-in-law phoned to say my twin sister's child had been born that very day. I have felt chill, horror and terror being communicated between people.

K: I suppose you'd be called middle-class now. How do you feel about claiming to write about working-class women?

R: Well, one of the topics in this new novel is money and class. My grandmother was working-class, she didn't die till she was ninety-nine, so I heard a lot of her remembered stories about working-class life. I'm examining what memory is and our imagination. The book is also about untruth - and telling the truth. My medium reckons she lived before, in ancient Egypt. Other characters think she's a fake.

K: When people claim to have lived before it's always in a hot climate.

R: Yes, not many want to have lived in the stone age, in the mud and the cold with dogs biting their legs. It's understandable that the imagination needs to think of a rich place for past rebirth. I do believe that places can soak up atmosphere and give it back to us powerfully.

K: Have you read any Buddhism?

R: A little, but not nearly enough. The whole question of reincarnation fascinates me; how far our atoms continue in another being. Reincarnation seems to be one way of describing genetics. I suppose that accounts for some of my interest in myth and religion; they describe in deep and symbolic ways what the body does, just as science attempts to grapple with life and death, and how one body decomposes, and how a new body comes together. Myth and science are two paths up the same mountain.

K: Do you find it difficult to write about sexuality?

R: One person's sensitive, deeply-felt text may be another person's pornography. That's why it's fun to read; we can quarrel about what's happening in a book. One person's pornography may not turn another person on at all. In <u>The Book of Mrs Noah</u> the narrator jokes that meat recipes turn her on.

K: Some critics might say it's irresponsible to turn someone on.

R: I don't think just describing the sexual act is necessarily irresponsible. It may be extremely boring. I like getting turned on.

K: What literature does that for you?

R: I've recently been reading Forster's short stories. They are about old men being turned on by young milkmen with huge dicks, whom they invite into their hotel, or to have a wonderful time in the bushes. Then the milkman goes back to his round, the narrator to his hotel. They are amusing, they are about sexual joy, meant for gay men perhaps, not aimed at women, but they turned me on.

K: What sort of language do you need to write well about sex?

R: You've got to make a literary decision: whether to use clinical, medical language, for example. That <u>could</u> be appropriate. Or do you use a riproaring pornographic language which seems to me very limited as it has about five words in it. Kathy Acker does that quite well, because she writes about sexual violence. She makes a critique of bourgeois culture, using words that we often think are revolting, to stress the boredom and despair of alienated sexuality, so that language works for her. Other people use more euphemistic language, and images which can sometimes say more.

It doesn't come naturally. You've got to work for it, it doesn't prove easy. You make a choice, a different choice each time, depending on your form and content.

K: Do you consider there is a wide difference between the way most men write and the ways women write?

R: For me it's inseparable that I'm a woman, a poet, and writer. Feminism is part of my bones and my blood. That presents difficulty - and pleasure.

K: Have your views changed?

R: Somewhat. I grew up with the Women's Movement, which liberated my anger. I was made to read so many male writers at university that for years afterwards I read mainly the women whose words had been almost forgotten till the eighties. They have given me enormous pleasure and stimulation. I needed to feel part of a Woman's tradition. But nowadays I'm able to see how modernism, for example, was used by both men and women in their different ways.

K: What books do you read by men?

R: I began re-reading men chronologically and now I'm reading autobiographies to try to understand how men feel - and I'm interested in the form. I think we can certainly extend our writing by learning from men.

K: Which are the male writers you particularly admire?

R: John Donne and Gerard Manley Hopkins.

K: And of those writing at the moment?

R: To my surprise I like Money by Martin Amis. He's looking at taboo area: his masculine self and pornography; it's brave and well done.

K: What is different in what women are doing?

R: Women are moving out of that period of modernism
when the preoccupation was with the breakdown of
language and form, the breakdown of the authorial
self into a new confidence. We are in a postmodernist,
confident phase; we are putting the bits together
again, working with the fragments, the splits and
breaks and making new myths.

K: That's what many Third World writers are doing.

R: I feel an affinity with them. We are at the heart of
society, though peripheralised. Without us, the culture
would fall apart. Blacks too have been marginalised,
like women, yet they are central to our culture. Their
labour has been essential to imperialism. As
imperialism falls apart, there's this great surge of
writing.

K: Who are the ones you most admire?

R: Toni Morrison and Alice Walker. Toni Morrison
makes myths out of everyday life in a way that's so
rich I feel humble.

K: Tell me about your most recent publication <u>Seven
Deadly Sins</u>.

R: This book was the brainchild of the editor Alison Fell.
But we all liked the title - and the idea of working
together again, and with a woman illustrating our
work.

K: Was it another collective venture like <u>Tales I Tell my
Mother</u>?

R: No, we each wrote separately, and didn't discuss them first. But when we read them we found there were exciting links and echoes and non-naturalistic metaphors.

K: You all start with the woman's body.

R: It's part of the reclaiming of our bodies for ourselves. When women take the body as starting point they are subverting a tradition of Western art. When I was a girl I felt I'd inherited a body which limited my meaning. Whereas middle-class boys could become priests, businessmen, anything they wanted, or saw other men do. There was a split between what my mind wanted, such as being a writer, and what society seemed to limit a girl's body to.

    I suppose it's almost inevitable that people respond to the body. In fact we find it difficult to respond to a person if we can't identify the gender. And the Seven Deadly Sins are physical as well as spiritual. It was rather exciting to write about sin.

K: Do you all see them in secular terms? After all, it's a religious concept.

R: Zoe Fairbairns wrote on covetousness. She did not see it in religious terms, but defended the covetous when the impoverished want more to live on. Her story is about whether an author should want more money. It's a topic of massive moral complexity because we all feel guilt about success. Women suffer this more than men.

K: You shouldn't feel guilty, it must be difficult living on a novelists earnings.

R: Yes, I only have about £4,000 a year.

K: The public should realise how little a writer gets if most of your time is spent struggling to improve, rather than journalism. Are short stories selling better these days?

R: Yes, they are becoming more popular, if they are in anthologies or structured round a theme. I like the openness that comes when there's no formal coherence but you're expanding the conception of genres by including many difference genres.

K: Tell me more about your story in <u>Seven Deadly Sins</u>.

R: Mine is about Anger. It has three different sources: firstly a tapestry in the Victoria and Albert museum. It's fifteenth-century, of a wild man and a wild woman, with lots of hair, very beautiful. Secondly, a newspaper article I read in Italy, about a folktale heroine called Melusina. She kills her father and turns into a monster-artist every Saturday night. Her husband is forbidden to spy on her, but he does, so loses her. And the third source was myself in the narrow fifties when it seemed monstrous for girls to want to be writers, and I felt a monster because I wanted to create.

K: How have you rewritten these?

R: I've taken the images these three sources offered me and set them in Provence, as a nineteenth-century fairy story. I make the husband a teacher who likes weirdos. He's heard about Melusine's change on Saturday nights, and wants to see her, touch her and then marry her. She is a damaged person; her mother dropped into the fire. We don't know whether it's by accident, or on purpose.

K: You seem to have changed the meaning of sin, like Brecht.

R: Sin is internalised by my heroine because she has grown up in a narrow-minded French Catholic culture - with a mother who felt it was wrong to have a woman's body and yet yearned to be an artist. If there is no way to struggle to express what we want with our bodies, if a patriarchal culture makes us feel our bodies are somehow wrong, if there is no language for the woman to express her conflicts, then hysteria can be the result.

K: Supposedly you write about sin, but in fact you are taking away the sense of sin.

R: We felt this was a chance to explore the shadowy parts of ourselves, and we enjoyed looking at the dark parts. These are not feminist heroines, they contain conflicts and clashes. I grew up under a cloud of guilt and found it liberating to <u>name</u> these sins.

K: Surely you all had a different approach?

R: It proved an interesting project precisely because we each had a different style and morality. It was liberating as we are so distinct formally. We did not read each other's; but since we all internalise sin, moving in there becomes problematic and demanding.

K: But surely taking the woman's body an metaphor need not be problematic?

R: That's true, but within Christian cultures we've lost the idea of the body as sacred. Which they had in ancient Egypt; perhaps one reason why my medium in my present novel imagines she once lived in ancient Egypt. It's a kind of wish-fulfillment, which I respect.

K: In <u>Wild Girl</u> you link a sense of the sacred with the woman's body?

R: Yes. Mary Magdalene has a full sexual life _and_ has spiritual visions.

K: Which I and my students found exciting and moving.

R: It's ironic that the Catholic church has no female saints who are sexual; none of them was allowed sexuality, only spirituality. I was writing the Fifth Gospel - according to Mary Magdalene, the outcast.

K: Would you have wished to be a priestess?

R: Yes - in a red robe, not a dog collar. But using the male language, the patriarchal vocabulary of theology would have been limiting as a woman.

K: You are writing in the stories of women who have been marginalised or used merely as images. Is that why you try to write as a working-class single mother in Tales I Tell my Mother?

R: At the time we were living in a squat in a working-class street. In fact their flats were much cleaner and tidier than ours. I'd refuse to write as a woman working in a sweatshop now. I think that story of mine was patronising and untrue.

K: Why? I liked the story, though it did not quite ring true.

R: You're right. I was _pretending_ to be that woman in the sweatshop behind Kings Cross station. For centuries women have been so colonised by men's imaginations; I don't think I have the right to do the same thing to working-class women. If I wrote about her now, it would have to be from the outside. I don't believe in character anyway.

K: I really enjoyed the way you made the women writers into symbols in Mrs Noah: the Babble-on Sybil, the

Confused Sybil, the Correct Sybil. Would you write about a black woman? They are under-represented in literature.

R: I'd refuse to now, because imperialism has represented them as it wanted, without reference to their feelings and experience. I'd want to excavate what black means to me, what racism means to me as a white woman. I couldn't invent a black character. Now black writers are telling what it means to them, with wonderful stories such as <u>Beloved</u> by Toni Morrison.

K: Her writing is full of rich images - not unlike yours. I wanted to ask you about how you even begin to structure a novel like <u>The Book of Mrs Noah</u>, with no plot and no story line?

R: It took a long time to write as I had no plan, only an image of riding into chaos. I found the structure by experimenting. You have to re-invent with each form. That takes time, endless drafts, effort and experiment.

K: Each of your forms is different, has its own distinct language. What criteria do you have for stopping a novel constructed of whirling images?

R: <u>Mrs Noah</u> took years of writing and rewriting. I found the form at last when I realised I wanted to interweave the stories of the five Sybils. Writing is a complex form of weaving. Or knotted string, with all the knots interconnecting. In fact the image I prefer is <u>plaiting</u>. There are five strands which are carefully woven into all the other parts, rather like a fishing net.

K: I like the image of plaiting, it's a female image, like Alice Walker's image of quilting: women picking up discarded bits and making them into a beautiful whole. Do you think women structure sentences differently from male writers?

R: Virginia Woolf did, she thought that Dorothy Richardson's long looping sentences are specifically 'feminine'. I'm not sure myself.

K: What do you think of Woolf's view that the writer is androgynous?

R: I now think that the writer should struggle to be bisexual and learn from the father as well as the mother. You have to start with your femaleness, <u>not</u> with writing like a man, and grow and expand from there, find your masculine part too. That takes <u>time</u>. But you must start with what you inherit: your sense of feminity, and explore all your anger and conflicts about that. If you jump straight into 'androgynous' writing, you're probably just pretending to be a man. I prefer the word 'bisexual': it's the <u>play</u> between the two sides that interests me, not some static state of rising above them.

K: What important differences still remain?

R: I think that women generally put more of themselves into their novels. And we seem to need to make connections. Perhaps because a woman working at home does about five things at once. Men classify more, systematise.

K: What advice have you for someone who is beginning to write? What advice do you give your Creative Writing Students?

R: I always say you need to write out of desire, out of your own longing to write, because of a yearning, or lack, or desire in yourself. Also you need to love language, to love words for their own sake, not use language just as a transparent medium for ideas.

emma

tennant

EMMA TENNANT was born in London in
  October 1937.

Novels	The Colour of Rain (as Catherine Aydy, 1964) The Time of the Crack (1973) The Last of the Country House Murders (1974) Hotel de Dream (1976) The Bad Sister (1978) Wild Nights (1979) Alice Fell (1980) Women Beware Women (1983)
Uncollected Short Stories	Mrs Ragley (Listener, 1973) Mrs Barratt's Ghost (New Statesman, 28 Dec. 1973) Philomela (Bananas, 1977) The Bed that Mick Built (New Stories 2, ed. Derwent May & Alexis Lykiard, 1977) Cupboard Love (in New Stories 4, ed. Elaine Feinstein & Fay Weldon, 1979) Tortoise-Shell Endpapers (Time Out, 21 Dec. 1979)
As Editor	Bananas (1977) Saturday Night Reader (1979)
Juvenile	The Boggart (1980)

K: You were very young when you began writing?

T: I was very young when I began telling stories, aloud, for myself, my dolls, anyone who would listen. In fact I only stopped when I heard my mother outside my door one day, whispering to some friends.

K: So you began in the oral tradition. When did you sit down to work out structure and plot?

T: Quite soon, because you must know the structure before you begin to write. A book can take you over, you know.

K: Do your characters sometimes take you over, as they do the lady novelist in Hotel de Dream?

T: Well, my approach is different in every novel. For example in my recent House of Hospitalities almost nothing happens because it concentrates entirely on character, on girls becoming women. I was very interested in girls' psychology while my two daughters were growing up. I read a lot of Bettelheim, and folklore about growing girls. In The Queen of the Stones one of the unhappy adolescents is inhabited by a poltergeist, but it's not treated from a feminist angle.

   What I often do with my characters is 'walk them up', as Henry James recommended. I walk them in this communal garden we share.

K: Can you carry on thinking out your novel while doing other things?

T: Not really. I'd recommend long weeks of tedium so that you've got time to live with the book. And time to write notes each evening, to help the next day's writing. You can't have too gay a social life.

K: What did you do when the children were small?

T: Paid for as much help as I could afford. It's only recently that women like myself can find the time to write _and_ have children.

K: Do you feel limited as a woman, as some feminists claim, because we are brought up using the male-dominated, patriarchal language which some people find constraining? How do you feel about the limitations in language?

T: I don't feel limited, though I probably should. I think my relationship with language is that I like to plunder from anywhere I possibly can; and as it all happens as I'm going along, I can't say I feel 'fear, shame and embarrassment' which Angela Carter feels. I can understand what it means. But I feel the point of writing for a woman is to take, magpie-like, anything they please from anywhere, and produce a subversive text out of the scraps; out of patriarchal or any kind of material they can get in their beaks.

K: I felt that in <u>The Adventures of Robina</u> and <u>Hotel de Dream</u> you take middle-class attitudes and implicitly criticise by putting them into some kind of fantasy or topsy-turvy world.

T: Yes, that was my intention. But a lot of people, unlike you, don't pick that up. They think you're writing something which is just comic or just entertaining. Not that I mind, because I have great admiration for anyone who can bring off comic writing. I sometimes think it's the greatest gift of all.

However you've hit it when you say my aim is to produce something subversive about the society in which we live. In <u>Hotel de Dream</u>, writing in a straightforward way, I'm showing dreams and fantasies of an England unable to bear the end of the Empire. Of course that was ten years ago, before the Falklands War. To write something like that now would demand a different cast. But still the same attitudes and feelings remain. We have not changed much, in the sense of grandiose failure.

K: Would you write something much blacker today?

T: Maybe, but I felt that the three so-called science fiction novels I wrote: <u>The Crack, The Last of the Country House Murders</u> and <u>Hotel de Dream</u> were oddly prophetic.

In <u>The Crack</u>, started in 1973, called <u>The Time of the Crack</u> by my publishers, the Southern, affluent half of England breaks off and floats toward Europe. I'd like to know what's happening now other than that.

In <u>Hotel de Dream</u> is an increasingly divided society, on the edge of being revolutionary, but unable at present to pull it off. And of course soaring property prices, landlords in seedy hotels, and the terrible bed-and-breakfast places we now see.

After I'd written <u>The Last of the Country House Murders</u> which is on a lighter note, what surprised me was to find eight years later that having invented the last of a dying aristocratic line who actually arranges his own murder for the sake of Japanese tourists, that there actually is a hotel like that. You can go to an expensive hotel, where you see the body, not in this case a real one, and you follow the clues, in 1930s Agatha Christie style. Again, heritage, English fantasy about its past, is something those three books deal with. They were intended to be strongly critical and satirical at the same time.

K: I thought it came off.

T: Oh, good. In <u>Robina</u>, my desire to use eighteenth-century pastiche was to show in 1985 that while Mrs Thatcher was proclaiming Victorian values, things had actually got so bad in this country that we had returned to eighteenth-century values, when there was little regard for human decency and you took your luck where you could find it. I use a type of <u>Moll Flanders</u> or <u>Roxana</u> (by Defoe) way of writing, I wanted to show that class of people in England who have become infinitely richer as a result of Tory government over the last eight or nine years. They never lost their extraordinary brutal way of going on, and must now be almost exactly like people in Smollett. Soon be going to own the coal mines again no doubt.

K: The quiet violence of those in power?

T: Yes, that's it.

K: But at the same time you really enjoyed writing it?

T: Yes, certainly I did. I thought the best way to get something like that over was to make it as funny as possible. After all you couldn't write an eighteenth-century pastiche and be leaden. It's got two faces, a comment on the aristocracy, which many people fail to take in. They still own about 90 per cent of the country. It's odd, as if there's some kind of given right. But in fact all these acres, owned by a few, puts them in a powerful position when a Thatcher government gains power. I remember hearing a landowner with vast lands on the borders of Scotland saying 'We've got the beef and we've got the bullets.' I put it in <u>The House of Hospitalities</u>, which is on that topic, though in a very different mode. That was many years ago of course, but I wouldn't be at all surprised if people weren't going on like that now.

K: And they still speak to you?

T: Not really, but occasionally a friend takes me into that world, where I listen to these strange statements and wonder 'What do they really mean?' Well, they mean they are like robber barons - that's what they're saying to each other. And I think of a photo I saw in The Independent of a town called Walkerburn on the borders of Scotland. It's near where I come from and almost everybody's been thrown out of work because of the woollen and textile mills being closed down. There are great hills in the distance, and on the left of the photograph the large house with pines all round it and a big wall. There you saw the out-of-work people's houses against the guarded, walled estate of the actual owner of the whole set-up. I used to know a lot of people who worked there.

K: There is a fantastic dichotomy between what you and I see of poverty, and what government representatives say about productivity rising. Virtually the only novel which discusses the social situation of the eighties is Margaret Drabble's The Radiant Way, which does it by piling on facts. Do you think that using elements of fantasy and the surreal would deal better with this topsy-turvy world?

T: Everyone has their own way of doing things. I couldn't do what Margaret Drabble does, which is probably extremely useful because there's nothing like facts and statistics. For a lot of readers, they're essential. But certain writers, among whom I'd count myself, looking at a kind of topsy-turvy society, use fantasy or allegory or science fiction as a way of getting through. By showing people in a completely different way what seems to be happening, and what looks likely to happen.

The reason why that way of writing started to catch on, mainly with younger people in the mid seventies, was because of a feeling of powerlessness and general impotence in the country. We felt at the same sort of a level as East European countries and South American dictatorships. When you cannot tell there's any real <u>terra firma</u> writers go into surrealism or into allegory to show the changeable, frightening, insecure and topsy-turvy world in which everybody lives.

K: Interesting that took off then, after the energy crisis which upset so many of our ideas about social improvement.

T: Quite true; in fact the opposite's happened.

K: It was wondering what forms you are experimenting with at the moment, because I know you are also interested in 'realism'.

T: In the year of <u>Midnight's Children</u> by Salman Rushdie (which I certainly admire) I happened to buy Angus Wilson's <u>Late Call</u>. Reading the two within a month, which I did, made me feel tremendous admiration for Angus Wilson's ability to deal with social change in a realistic and moving way.

The trouble with these things is that they're <u>all</u> true. On the one hand, surrealism and allegory, if it's good, is important; on the other hand there must be writers who can write as Angus Wilson did. But it's hard now, as things are changing so fast, to be able to write about the <u>present</u>. I was trying to think, apart from Zola, who can? Balzac often went back thirty years and then sometimes came up to the present. But he went back a lot - what's the answer? Was it because for years the franc scarcely changed its value so there was greater sense of stability?

K: Who were the main influences on you? Surely not Zola and Balzac?

T: The main influences were Latin American, Marquez of course. But above all East European, particularly Bruno Shultz, whom I think everybody would enjoy very much indeed. He only wrote two novels, both of which I think are still in print. His <u>Street of Crocodiles</u> is one of the most extraordinary novels, which to <u>me</u> seem more extraordinary than Kafka. Great germs, great seed beds for my books <u>Wild Nights</u> and <u>Alice Fell</u>. A whole new way of looking at things was opened up by him. It's very important for someone who is studying writing to read him.

K: What advice have you for adults who want to write?

T: Experiment in different genres. One of the important things to say about writing, to people who are starting to write, is that most depressing squashing of confidence is to feel that there is not a channel for <u>you</u>. Of course at first you don't know how to say what you want to say. In the old days people used to say 'I haven't got a voice yet, I can't find it.' The answer is that there are <u>hundreds</u> of voices. But you have to read them and hear them to find which will take you into the thing you want to say. I think it's been destructive in the past that there has to be just <u>one</u> voice and if you can't find it, you've had it and you're a failure.

K: How did you feel when Alberto Moravia publicly burnt your first novel?

T: Terrible, but thanks to the great plurality of what's been happening since the mid seventies, when all this writing from other countries has been available, and translated, we are freer to tackle other genres. As with clothes, now people wear clothes from each succeeding era. Writing has opened out too, and it's frightening and odd in one way; but tremendously encouraging for finding what you want to express and a way you want to express it. And these writers - Marquez is obviously a tremendous thing for people and Borges is obviously a tremendous thing and there are enough amazing Egyptian writers too to suggest different ways of writing. One book I enjoyed immensely was by Mariama Ba - So Long a Letter. She's not an influence on me, I wish I had the talent to be. She wrote only one great novel before she died.

K: Who else influenced you?

T: If I had not been helped by J.G. Ballard as a person and especially as a writer, I'd have been stuck permanently in trying to write realist novels which never worked. I did publish a short novel in dialogue when I was twenty-five. After that I got completely stuck, because there appeared to be only one naturalist mode. I didn't dare show my writing to anybody. It's now infinitely easier, since about 1972, because I've had the luck to meet writers who've said, 'Come on, you don't have to do what you think you have to do. Structure a thing in the following way and don't be too grand, write it.'

I realised, not that I was grand, but that people teaching you were suggesting you had to try and be as good as Henry James or Proust. That's the killer. Forget it. I had a horrible time for eight or nine years after my first novel came out. I got various jobs in journalism.

K: Would you advise would-be writers to try journalism?

T: For those who want to write novels, my advice is forget the attempt to understand life through literature. In most cases you'll be stuck and unhappy. Choose a genre, if you are stuck, and you'll find that when deciding to do a thriller you may have an excellent ear for dialogue in contemporary life, and you may be telling people something important. Or use fantasy or science fiction and what you really think about things may well come out in that way. Don't be too posh.

K: You try a different form in every novel?

T: That's my multiple personality. It doesn't give me many sales. I don't want to moan, but the new Brookner or the new Murdoch is relatively similar to the last, and readers know roughly what to expect, and they buy.

What I found was that having met talented sci-fi writers, and having done three novels using elements of sci-fi, I then felt free to go off and explore different directions.

K: I enjoyed the different direction of <u>The Queen of the Stones</u>, with its excerpts from newspapers interspersed with sections of poetic prose.

T: There's one thing I think about poetic prose: that you can't do too much of it. You can write maybe two novels. But it's a bit of a dead end, so you've got to pull yourself out of that. You can't really go on like Djuna Barnes, though I don't compare myself to her, or writers like that, but they never do many. A distinctive poetic voice is probably about two novels followed by a depressed silence.

K: Some do it well, such as Eva Figes or Elaine Feinstein.

T: Elaine's a great friend of mine. I think <u>The Border</u> is marvellous. She's had a tough time.

K: She tells me she finds other women very supportive these days. Have you found that too? I certainly have.

T: I think that there can be no woman writer around who

doesn't feel that if it hadn't been for the Women's Movement, they might well find themselves in the position of Sylvia Plath. One can use it as help and bulwark, that's what the whole Movement is for. It supports me as an individual _and_ as a writer.

K: Women are reading and publishing more by women, has this helped you as a novelist?

T: I must be the only one whose sales haven't increased, partly by always jumping into different categories, from one genre to another. If I'd been a feminist woman writer like Angela Carter...

K: What has not helped you then?

T: If I decide I'll write something about an upper middle-class milieu, then all the people who liked The Bad Sister think I'm writing about a disgusting subject. Too many reviewers think in categories. A naive left-wing person wouldn't read me then, though I may well have something critical about a milieu they dislike.

It's an odd life, completely split. When The Bad Sister comes out again, there will be nothing about it in the right wing press. I have just written a new book The Strange Case of Ms Jekyll and Mrs Hyde which I hope is good. It was difficult to do.

K: You are influenced by Scottish writers, aren't you?

T: Yes, especially James Hogg. I grew up in his part of the country, the same part he came from. In fact his 'most enchanted wood' was opposite my bedroom window. Where people were turned into threelegged stools and fairy rings.

The whole subject of the double came into Britain via Scotland and German metaphysics, Hoffmann and others. It didn't take in England, the idea of the doppelganger. The reason was that then England was solid and Scotland was split - between two languages, split between being Scottish and being English. It took root in Scotland with Hogg's The Confessions of a Justified Sinner, a masterpiece. It inspired me to write The Bad Sister, a sort of feminist response to Justified Sinner.

And Stevenson was utterly receptive to the 'double' in both Dr Jekyll and Mr Hyde and The Master of Ballantrae. I think it's Scottish to be split, to talk in one way and have to go South to make your living. This brought about the 'double' taking root there.

Now that England is split between an aircraft landing ground for America and not knowing what it is, these new kinds of writing are causing excitement here. Whether they are Indian, or satirical, like Bulgakov's The Master and Margarita, or Golding's Lord of the Flies.

K: His novel came to my mind when I reread your The Queen of Stones. Was it an answer to Golding?

T: Yes, I was saying 'There's The Lord of the Flies about the myths that sustain boys. Here's a novel about young girls' myths.' Myths about witches, about nurses, about abandonment.

K: But The Queen of the Stones is not in a wholly mythical register. You open with a newspaper account of young girls lost in the fog.

T: It was wholly made up. Though it took some critics in, who read it like Truman Capote's In Cold Blood.

K: It found it an exciting read, with so many different discourses. Has it sold well?

T: Not particularly. Both Jonathan Cape and Faber and Faber consider that a good novel should sell itself; whereas a newer, smaller publisher, like Viking, works hard at publicity and consequently sells more of the novels it promotes.

K: Perhaps it's also the subject-matter? You analyse the psyche of young girls, a topic which fascinates feminist literary critics.

T: That's true. And for years I read a lot of Laing etc. I think one's got to try to find oneself as a woman if you want to create. I read a great many books such as The Yellow Wallpaper by Charlotte Perkins Gilmore, The Female Malady and lots more. They have all helped me to write by showing me how we've been classified in patriarchal society. You have to look at the whole history of female insanity, in what way women are driven mad and how much it's the fault of society, of false classification. In three novels I look at the psychology of growing girls. The Queen of the Stones was my first stab at looking at girls' responses.

K: And what are you stabbing at now?

T: I'm embarked on a gigantic book, rather like The Queen. In fact it should be finished fairly soon as I have a wonderful rapid typist, who, as it happens, worked for Laing for years.

K: Which other women novelists interest you?

T: I've just been reading a good new thriller writer, Joan Smith. I think women are doing something really interesting with the detective novel at the moment - taking it further than P.D. James or Ruth Rendell, though they are good in a more traditional way. Joan Smith's 'A Masculine Ending' is interesting and so is the American Valerie Miner's Murder in the English

<u>Department</u>, set in Berkeley.   She's a youngish feminist.

K: What books would you take on a summer holiday?

T: All twelve volumes of Proust's <u>Remembrance of Things Past</u> are the best holiday reading I know. Much less agitating than Dostoevsky, far more exciting than Trollope, it can go to the beach in singles or pairs, the translation by Terence Kilmartin enhancing the pleasure of visiting or revisiting Francoise, Albertine, Saint-Loop and Marcel. The washed skies of Ballbec will transport you from the crude Aegean blue and the panelled houses of Proust's atrocious aristocracy remove some of the pain of the sun-blistered picnic by the sea.

   My second choice is Maya Angelou's outstanding autobiography.   The story of an extraordinarily courageous and humane life is told with humour, wit and tenderness. These volumes speak also of a search for justice after cruelty, and of identity after struggle. Start with <u>I Know Why the Caged Bird Sings</u> and go on from there.

K: And what are you writing at the moment?

T: Last year the sequel of <u>House of Hospitalities</u> was published. It's called <u>A Wedding of Cousins</u>. And this year Faber brings our <u>Two Women of London: The Strange Case of Ms Jekyll and Mrs Hyde</u>. At the moment I'm engrossed in another, but prefer not to talk about it, in case I feel I have to change it a great deal.

fay

weldon

FAY WELDON was born in Worcestershire in 1933

Novels	The Fat Woman's Joke (1967)
	Down Among the Women (1971)
	Female Friends (1975)
	Remember Me (1976)
	Little Sisters (1978)
	Praxis (1978)
	Puffball (1980)
	Watching Me, Watching You (1981)
	The President's Child (1982)
	The Lives and Loves of a She Devil (1984)
	The Shrapnel Academy (1986)
	The Heart of the Country (1987)
	The Heart and Lives of Men (1987)
	The Rules of Life (1987)
	Leader of the Band (1988)
Short Stories	Polaris and Other Stories (1985)
Non Fiction	Letters to Alice on First Reading Jane Austen (1985)
	Rebecca West (1985)
Juvenile	Wolf the Mechanical Dog (1988)

K: Do you mind giving interviews and talking about yourself?

W: I still have difficulty in beginning sentences with 'I' as I was told so often as a child, when writing letters, that one should never start with 'I'. But I'll tell you briefly what people expect to know about women: their marital status. I am married, I have four children, all boys, one over thirty, the youngest still at primary school, so you can make a quick deduction about my age from that.

K: Have you always lived in London?

W: I have a rather confused background, some of my family were writers, some musicians. As a small child I was brought up in New Zealand by my mother, in a fairly working-class way. It was a totally female household, with grandmother - and I attended a girls' school. It never occurred to me that men make most decisions till I went out into the world. In the fifties I did not argue with this. One of the causes of our unhappiness is the desire to change what is wrong. When I was a girl you just accepted society without changing it, you accepted that your life would be in the home. Though only in theory, since so many women had to work in practice.

K: Is that why you began writing novels?

W: The kind of woman who writes novels is usually comfortably brought up, goes to university, and has enough time and leisure and money to write without much urgency. For me simple survival was difficult, I could not begin till I was over thirty, and only then because I had a job in advertising. I had children and was wearing myself out, but in the sixties you pretended you could manage. I began to get rather angry, and this sense of injustice led me to write. Of course the Womens Movement had existed for over two hundred years, but had gone underground. I actually got a degree in economics without knowing what 'rates' are - which seems indicative of the sort of teaching we got.

K: So your apprenticeship was in copy writing?

W: I had always earned my living by writing - in advertising agencies, or market research; I had brief stints writing reports, propaganda, in the Foreign Office, and answering letters for <u>The Daily Mail</u> and <u>Daily Mirror</u>. I earned a miserable pittance at all these jobs, except advertising, when I started writing television adverts and then TV scripts in the mid sixties.

K: How did you break into what was considered a male, technological area?

W: I began with TV adverts, so I learned the layout of scripts and got used to hearing about camera angles. Having written television commercials, I realised how to put down what I wanted, so it held no mystery for me.

K: Surely in the mid sixties it was seen as a male occupation?

W: There certainly was a mystique, a feeling that women could not write in dramatic form. Women seldom attempted the theatre either. And it is difficult to learn to write in dramatic form, you can either tell stories in dialogue or not, the way some people can draw.

K: What else motivated you to attempt this 'male' preserve?

W: Indignation and the knowledge that there was an enormous amount to be said. Women's lives are as interesting as men's - if not more so - and nobody seemed to realise this. Once I started there was a responsive audience, because if you are thinking this on your own, then you come in on a wave of energy to discover many others are thinking in the same way. When I wrote The Fat Women's Tale for TV, I had to cut so much, which hurt, that I took to the novel. It gives total control over the minds of your characters - and no designer doing things wrong. My early novels started mainly as stage or television plays. With me a story grows through dialogue, then you give it flesh and blood. From novels I progressed to short stories. Mostly because I was asked.

K: When did you learn how to tackle short stories, which can be even more complex than novel-writing?

W: I never learned. In fact when a professor of American literature moved in next door, he explained I was doing it all wrong, that stories and characters have to be developed, that it's impossible to open with eight characters on the first page, which I do. I suppose that if I had tried to learn the theory I'd have had far more trouble; all I wanted to do was communicate. Then you get asked to do things. A friend of mine was editor of an annual anthology of ghost stories. If other writers let him down he would ask me to produce a tale of the occult for next Tuesday. If I seem to have a preoccupation with mystery, that's partly why. But he wouldn't have asked me if I hadn't a sense of a reality behind a reality.

K: Many people would like to know how a mother of four children finds time to write.

W: My husband cooks, and I don't clean. You should see the house. Once you start earning you can pay someone else to help with the children. But it does require physical strength and energy; and other people's requirements of you. When an editor rings up angrily giving me a deadline, I meet it.

K: Did you find any difficulty in getting published?

W: Fairly little, as far as I can remember. But the mood was different in the sixties, we didn't seem to mind about getting into print. Though my first play did take two years to get on. I was not accustomed in those days to taking myself seriously. My first play had a man as its central character - with a woman they might not have done it.

My second was funny, so they didn't notice it was serious. Then you learn what you are doing as other people tell you.

K: Do you discuss it with your family?

W: No, I discourage them. They don't really want to know. Men certainly don't want to have these edgy, complaining, ungracious, miserable women writing in their lives. What you do is their misfortune, so you'd better not rub it in. It must be terrible for wives of male writers too.

K: Do you feel you can write whatever you want?

W: Yes, I take things to the edges of credibility.

K: And what do your publishers say when you submit your manuscript?

W: The word 'Submit' is deplorable - who do they think they are? You listen to what they say, as you listen to professors of literature. But in the end you are the arbiter, and do what <u>you</u> think best.

K: Lorna Sage states that you are no longer trying to mediate between men and women, but see more difference than ever before.

W: In advertising I was intensely conscious of the way we are sold a notion or normality. I want to take that process apart.

K: Many people find that process bleak.

W: But there's a kind of cheerfulness in facing up to the savagery of the truth. There are too few writers who are preoccupied with the actual state of the world. It's unfortunate that novelists are professionals who think 'Now I'll write a novel,' instead of thinking what there is to be said - and if there's nothing, shut up. I never run out of things to say.

K: Can you teach people how to write?

W: You can save people from a couple of years' struggling. Of course people who are ambitious and determined will write. There are no rules, each case is different - and good Creative Writing courses can help.

K: Some writers, like Emma Tennant, say the most difficult thing is to be funny, do you agree?

W: I'd rather be serious than funny. But humour is a sort of punctuation, one funny sentence saves two paragraphs of serious intent. An amusing line will hurry you on to your deadline. The bare facts of our life are so grim and grisly, because we're all going to die. That's hard enough to put up with, so there has to be some kind of pleasure, some kind of animation in our response to daily life; it's all we have and should be reflected in the novels we read.

K: Why do you think we read novels?

W: Our lives seem chaotic, though we try to impose some pattern on experience; now novels impose a pattern with beginning, middle and end, and some kind of moral. They develop out of children's stories, and give us the illusion that shape and order is possible.

K: If you impose too much of your own shaping, you may produce stereotyping. Do you use stereotype because you want to talk about as many types of women as possible, as many kinds of women's experience as possible?

W: I don't think I set out to do that, it may be my ineptness that they seem caricature. The way things come at you is so different from one person to another. I find people in real life more like caricatures than they suspect, such as solicitors, or any of the professions. I believe that people fall into patterns, though they probably don't.

K: Do you see different patterns in the novels men are producing?

W: Less and less, because men are beginning to write the sort of novels that women have been writing for the last ten years. They now understand that power, male identity crises, and war are absurd things to write about and are now looking at human relationships. There is a younger generation of male writers trying to come to terms with the world, to look at at clearly without heroes - or heroines. It took the latest wave of women's writing to escape from the loving, caring gentle mode and tell the truth, as some men also do, like Martin Amis in <u>Money</u> or Malcolm Bradbury.

K: Your first novel <u>A Fat Women's Joke</u> dealt with women's bodies and the way women see food as comfort and enemy. Do you write mainly for women?

W: I don't consciously write for women. I'm preoccupied with women's state in the world and feel men should look after themselves. Men are welcome to read me - and do so in increasing numbers. My process is to discover something in fiction and hand it over. I feel I'm a processor of ideas, and if one does this with skill and integrity then people are going to want to read it. I write the sort of books I want to read.

K: I certainly noticed male reviewers were interested in Puffball. Can you explain why, as it's so much about your reactions to pregnancy?

W: It's partly fantasy and partly folklore; and perhaps they are interested because it's also a study in opposite: town and country; cold and heat; doctor and witchwoman. These two are dealing in the same substances, but in a rather different way. Science actually saves my heroine after magic has almost destroyed her. There is a level of truth we all respond to in our worst moments.

K: Are you criticised for writing too much about subjects such as illness?

W: You write about what currently obsesses or interests you. I suppose I could become typecast, but I diverge strongly from what you expect: Puffball is about the sanctity of motherhood which is not a particularly progressive or popular theme.

K: Where do your themes come from?

W: Things are bound to come at you from television and the newspapers, in our society. You write out of a society, and it's changing all the time. I write out of the flux; you don't set out to write about this or that. Afterwards, people tell you what your themes are, and you may well agree.

K: How much do you listen to the criticism of your work?

W: I don't think one can always ignore everything that departments of literature say. Yet, simply because novels are so long and require one's own animation, one cannot listen too much. I remain slightly mystified by what critics say the novel ought to be. It seems to me that a novel is anything you can persuade a publisher to print - and readers to read. When I was in Australia, teaching Creative Writing for a term, they complained that my short stories are not really short stories as they do not conform. I could only agree. Nevertheless they had read them so I ended with a definition as 'something which stops rather quickly.'

K: Did you feel out on a limb?

W: Yes often. And I was told my stage plays show bad manners as they usually have a small cast with few people. Now, recently I worked with Ann Jellicoe who wants two hundred people on the stage at a time, in her Community theatre. You have to know what you want. Henceforth I shall be careful not to have less than two people on the stage at a time.

K: How did your audiences change?

W: More people seem to read each novel I write. My first novels were gratifying to me, surprising to some, shocking to many. When I began people would walk out of rooms, judging my books as indecent and subversive. Today they are not particularly surprising as all these ideas are in common circulation. So I'm going off into a more literary area, less indignant, because so many others are doing it well, probably better than me. I lament the single-minded feeling I had that the solution to world problems lay with women. I thought that if the potential of women were released into society it would instantly transform itself. Now we see that the picture is more confusing than we realised - or hoped.

K: In <u>Praxis</u> the interludes about decay reminded me of Beckett.

W: It wasn't another writer who influenced me, but what I see. Death faces all of us. And most of us, especially women, are going to end our lives alone and ill. But I rescue Praxis and give her a couple of years more.

K: I like that ending - how far do you plan those final twists?

W: You don't know - because it's a game; when you arrive near the end, you realise what could have happened.

K: So at the end of <u>Down Among the Women</u> we discover it's Jocelyn who's written the story.

W: Yes, I realised she could be reformed. I enjoy playing games; the most complicated game was <u>The Little Sisters</u>.

K: Do you know the endings of your novels before you begin writing?

W: No. Sometimes you know more clearly if you start with a premiss to consider. In a way <u>Praxis</u> was the working out of a word. How much is conscious how much unconscious I don't know. About the third of the way through a novel I realise what it's about, what the resolution is. Then it's easier to get where you want, though it varies from novel to novel. All writers proceed differently. I am about to start another now and I'm just terrified.

K: Do you enjoy reading <u>other</u> people's books?

W: Yes, I enjoy reading novels - some for diversion, some to see what other writers are doing, some knowing you are going to hate them, some you admire. A good novel takes all your time and attention. Sometimes one hasn't the moral or emotional energy to read with more than half your mind.

K: You set your paragraphs out differently than most, with gaps. Why?

W: Because I started writing in televison where you begin something new by leaving a gap. Also because I did a lot of copywriting when you have to fight for every word as the typographer is there telling you how difficult it is for readers to absorb blocks of copy. This has gone so far now that probably the converse may be true.

K: Would you have written like this if you hadn't worked in advertising?

W: I cannot say, but there are others who do it.

K: Did your pregnancies make you want to write fast?

W: No. I felt well with all the oestrogen - and being rooted to the spot helped. <u>Puffball</u> was written soon after I became pregnant as it related to an actual experience. It was written deliberately fast because the feelings of being pregnant evaporate so quickly and the whole pattern of physical changes disappears months after you've had them. That novel was an attempt to nail them.

K: Do you have the illusion that you are controlling your reader?

W: Well, I took to the novel instead of the theatre because you have more control; but I fail, partly because of the length of time that it takes to write. In contrast you seem to be writing merely a blueprint for television, and others change it as they see fit.

K: Have you written for radio?

W: Yes, it's a lovely form because you communicate through people's ears and you create a whole world as you wish it to be.

K: Do you like reviewing?

W: Only the books which I really enjoy, so I'm not much use.

K: Many critics did not enjoy <u>The Life and Loves of a She-Devil</u>.

W: Some applauded as she turns herself into a sex object, happy ever after.

K: Do you take criticism on board?

W: In <u>Praxis</u> I tried to remove my remarks from the narrative. Though it's part of my pleasure to direct myself to the reader. You are not in theory supposed to do it too much; I also cut out many of the funny lines, so it was taken more seriously. But to keep myself in the book, I had the story related by an old woman; the commentary was removed from the main text, and fitted in chunks into Praxis herself. I wrote the end in hospital, waiting for my baby to be born. About a hundred pages from the end the pace seems to speed up, because I was writing uninterrupted, trying to get it finished in time.

K: So that's how you find the time most women can't.

W: If you really want to do it enough and there's something

you want to say, you work on the principle that children sleep more than you do. You get up two hours earlier every morning. Some things simply have to be given up. I was in Russia recently and our translator had a small baby and a job and wanted to carry on writing. I asked her when he got up and she answered four in the morning, so I could hardly suggest she got up at two. Sometimes it's impossible and you have to wait twenty years.

But you have to keep your hand in. A difficulty about writing prose is that it requires training from a young age to express your thought in written words on the page. Vague thoughts flitting through your head have to be nailed down. You start off groping for words, then it gets a little easier and you manage to get more complex thoughts down - that is how style develops. A woman has to keep at it while looking after children. In America they seem to think you can't have both. I think having children and an interest in painting and music are all part of the same creative energy, a desire to create something new where there was nothing before.

K: How do you decide on the form that's most appropriate?

W: That depends on what ideas you've got in your head, sometimes it may be a stage play because there are a few things you can only say on the stage.

K: Why do you prefer the novel in spite of your success with TV plays?

W: That form is limited by time and what cameras can do - and there's simply more to be said. If you want to say more you are going to have to ask people to read it. But you don't sit down and decide 'Now I'm going to try the novel form'; if you're me you don't even sit down and say 'Now I'm going to write a novel.' Though I have to sometimes now, as publishers keep saying 'Where is your novel?' And I answer 'In my head.' To which they reply 'That's not good enough.'

K: Do you still find it difficult to clear time to write?

W: Once I began to earn enough at advertising I could afford to pay a laundry to do the washing - a machine would have disturbed the male ego. And I began to use taxis, because that's twenty minutes saved when you can write a page. Money makes life much easier, I use it to make time.

K: David Lodge praises your short staccato paragraphs, like advertising.

W: It was never my intention to write traditional novels - or even novels. I just wanted to get something down in fictional form, and had very little time and a great deal to say. I think it's the shortage of time which makes my novels take the form they did. You make your points as fast as you can - that's where humour helps. One comic sentence can replace a page.

K: Are you able to write regularly each day?

W: No, I write in bursts, or to meet deadlines. Occasionally I go off to a hotel room and shut myself up till I'm finished. Stage plays have to be written like that, with a concentrated flow of thought. You cannot have any other life in the middle.

K: How soon were you able to start supporting yourself?

W: I did not write the novels with any hope of making money. Initially you have to write a novel just because you want to, not because you need to support yourself, which is probably why they get taken seriously. They are seen as a truer artistic expression than television, which is done to make money. Once you sell abroad and go into paperback, novels begin to pay, but it takes time. As television is well paid it took me only a year to earn enough from that to live on.

K: I have just re-read your <u>Letters to Alice, on First Reading Jane Austen</u>. You are so different from the Austen tradition of crafting novels, what is it that you particularly admire in her? Her wit? Her concision?

W: I like the whole, and she's such fun. I hadn't re-read her since I left school and I enjoyed adapting <u>Pride and Prejudice</u> for television.

K: You certainly did it with love, your adaptation caught her spirit. Tell me more about the dedication to that book. You wrote 'To my mother to whom I owe such morality and wisdom as I have.'

W: My mother is an intellectually rigorous person, and she is extremely well read. Everything that happened when I was a child was put in some moral context, though not a conventional one. She would show us that nothing is wholly good or bad, neither our actions nor other people's.

K: So she gave you a training in scepticism?

W: Yes, not just about the outside world but about one's own nature. It was never 'Don't do this' but 'It would be wiser if you don't do this because.' So you grew up with a capacity to make your own decisions. I daresay it's what you would develop in a religious household, but then the do's and don'ts would be linked with religious ritual, to conventional right and wrong, which is not the same. Easier but less productive.

K: Do you think that upbringing made you more aware? Your books often tell women they are too unaware of what they are doing to themselves.

W: Yes, it was a training in that, which comes out strongly in <u>Female Friends.</u> Those three friends are anti-heroines, who have to learn not to be exploited, that to forgive and forget is often unwise.

K: Was it your mother who taught you goodness is seldom rewarded?

W: That became evident fairly early. I can't recall any suggestion that you did good in order to be rewarded. Goodness is something you aspire to, though even some great fiction, like Jane Austen's, echoes the belief 'If you are good you will be happy.' The discovery that no amount of goodness prevents disaster has thrown many people into despair, depression and even death. Perhaps even Jane Austen herself, dying unrewarded of Addison's disease. The relationship between death and the auto-immune system is not the mystery it once was.

K: As you emphasise when you state in <u>Praxis</u> that nature is our enemy, giving us cancer, polyps, headaches. May I ask you about <u>The Leader of the Band</u>? You make the heroine's father an SS doctor, shot for war crimes, and she is the product of genetic engineering. Isn't that too great a burden for one person?

W: I think it's the burden we all carry; in fact she's everyone because she has a history of insanity, of war crimes, of the general behaviour of nations, and she's trying to make sense of it.

K: Where did this particular novel have its origins?

W: I went off with a band round France.

K: But you have not been subjected to genetic engineering.

W: In France I was thinking about places where the war still seemed to be a living memory; and I realised how much it is in everybody, so this woman has been made by war.

K: She tries to escape by going from man to man. How far do you feel at ease creating male characters?

W: I feel at liberty to invent women, as I'm female. I merely describe men. It's hard to avoid stereotyping, but there are a lot of good male novelists around, I'll leave that to them.

K: You make many oracular comments here and in The Shrapnel Academy. You speculate, you prophesy; is this a tempting role?

W: Of course, and why not? Who else is there to do it? I don't expect to be agreed with. But when people turn to the novel, they are looking for some sort of moral framework which they can apply to their own lives. It is comforting to have a vision of the world in which good is rewarded and evil is punished.

K: You are extraordinarily prolific. This is your eighth novel in three years, as well as seven television plays. Could there be a danger in such facility?

W: Prolific is not a respectable thing for any writer to be. I could reply by saying that others read too slowly, not that I write too fast.

K: What advice have you for aspiring writers?

W: At first I was terrified, and thought I ought to cut. I began on a typewriter because I thought that's what other writers did - certainly Graham Greene does.

Then I started to use a felt-tipped pen; it gives you a space between thought and language. It helps develop your style, gives space for adjectives, so you can amplify as you go along. Then you decide that if a thing is worth an adjective it's worth a sentence.

K: Is that why your style is more flowing in The President's Child?

W: That's a matter of decision, there are three different styles, here's a domestic one, a thriller and the poetic interludes.

K: You are much more planned and deliberate than you sometimes admit. Are there awful days when your writing won't go right?

W: The desire to get words right absorbs me. Days differ, but you just have to keep going. I'm quite good at keeping plots in my head. And I make chance play a large part in my plots as it does in life. You are free. And if you give up the desire for a good self-image, then you can invent the terrible things I make my She-devil do.

K: Do you think women have a greater potential to be free than men?

W: It's hard to tell as so few have it. If you removed the conditioning, I suspect we'd be much the same. Once differences become less, I'll be able to invent male characters more easily. What's exciting at the moment is that women writers are not only changing our view of character, they are changing our very language.

further

reading

All books are published in London, unless otherwise indicated.

USEFUL GENERAL CRITICISM

M. Bradbury, Possibilities: Essays on the State of the Novel 1973, OUP
The Novel Today 1977, Fontana. This contains Murdoch, 'Against
Dryness' and Lodge, 'The Novelist at the Crossroads'.

 The Contemporary English Novel 1979, Arnold. This includes Byatt
'People in Paper Houses', and Sage, 'Female Fiction'.

A. Burgess, The Novel Now 1967, Faber. Burgess is wide-ranging and
idiosyncratic, with a perceptive chapter on women.

D.J. Enright, A Mania for Words 1984   Enright takes a traditional
approach. He includes a short article on the female, The Tale of Genji.

B. Hardy, The Appropriate Form 1964, Tellers and Listeners 1975
(both Athlone Press). Perceptive writing from a woman critic who was
Leavisite, but appreciates aspects of modern theory.

R. Jackson, Fantasy 1983, Methuen. She uses new criticism incisively.

G. Josipovici, The World and the Book 1971, Macmillan. Josipovici
introduces French criticism (especially Barthes), imaginatively, with
essays on Proust, Dante and the rise of the novel.

D. Lodge, The Language of Fiction adapts modern criticism. Working
with Structuralism 1981, Routledge and Kegan Paul. Lodge does not
provide a thorough introduction, but he approaches the topic for a
beginner.

W. Ong, Orality and Literacy 1982, Methuen. Ong presents an
imaginative, erudite study of the oral traditions of the working-class
and women.

C. Rawling ed., Popular Fiction and Social Change contains a seminal
article on science fiction by M. Jordin, 1984, Macmillan.

J.P. Sartre, What is Literature? 1965, Harper Colophon N.Y. Worth re
reading.

T. Tanner, City of Words: American Fiction 1950-70 1971, Cape.
Tanner states that 'a novel should be able to contain in language our
destiny'.

A. Wilson, <u>Diversity and Depth</u> 1984, Secker and Warburg. Angus Wilson has collected a good range of his reviews, on <u>Clarissa</u>, Camus, Murdoch, Claude Simon and many others.

A useful reference work is <u>Contemporary Novelists</u> 1982, St Martins Press N.Y. It offers brief accounts of the novels and bibliographies, as does <u>The Oxford Companion to English Literature</u> ed. Margaret Drabble 1985.

CONTEMPORARY CRITICISM

Catherine Belsey <u>Critical Practice</u> 1980, Methuen. This text provides the best written brief introduction to theories of Barthes and Derrida.

Roland Barthes, <u>Mythologies</u> 1972, Cape. These fascinating, concise, approachable essays use his sign system to analyse myths, books, even wrestling. Read <u>S/Z</u>, 1975 Cape, for his analysis of Balzac's realism.

<u>A Barthes Reader</u> ed. Susan Sontag, 1985, Cape, provides a brilliant, idiosyncratic introduction, putting him in an older French tradition.

Jonathan Culler, <u>On Deconstruction: Theory and Criticism after Structuralism</u> 1982, Cornell Univ. Press. Culler is erudite and helpful.

Terry Eagleton, <u>Myths of Power, a Marxist Study of the Brontes</u> 1975, Macmillan. This offers a perceptive introduction to marxist criticism. Then read his thorough <u>Marxism and Literary Theory</u> 1976, Methuen. One of the most reliable introductions to recent theory is his paperback <u>Literary Theory</u> 1983, Blackwell Oxford. Eagleton is a major contemporary critic.

Terence Hawkes, <u>Structuralism and Semiotics</u> 1977, Methuen. Hawkes offers a historical introduction, clear exposition and annotated bibliography.

Richard Kearney, <u>The Wake of the Imagination (Ideas of Creativity in Western Culture)</u> Winter 1987, Hutchinson. This Irish philosopher writes on modern French theory enthusiastically. He points out that postmodernism need not relinquish all humanism if it respects the ethical imagination.

Pierre Macherey, <u>A Theory of Literary Production</u> 1978, Routledge and Kegan Paul. This is a demanding text by a leading Marxist.

David Punter, <u>The Hidden Script: Writing and the Unconscious</u> 1985, Routledge. Punter offers an illuminating, uneven investigation of the unconscious in Carter, Lessing, Bainbridge, Ballard and others.

Bernard Bergonzi, <u>The Myth of Modernism and Twentieth Century Literature</u> 1985, Harvester. He relates literature to its cultural context.

Raman Selden, <u>A Reader's Guide to Contemporary Literary Theory</u> 1980, Harvester. Professor Selden expounds theory from Bakhtin and Lukacs to Foucault and Kristeva, with guides for further reading.

FEMINIST LITERARY CRITICISM

The most helpful introductions are:

The <u>New Feminist Criticism</u> ed. Showalter 1986, Virago. Professor Showalter includes many pathbreaking recent articles.

<u>Making a Difference</u> ed. Greene and Kahn. 1985, Methuen. This collection includes essays on varieties of feminist criticism, American, French, black and Lesbian criticism.

Maggie Humm, <u>Feminist Criticism: Women as Contemporary Writers</u> 1986, Harvester. Humm explores contemporary theory and its effect on women writers.

Toril Moi, <u>Sexual/Textual Politics</u> 1986, Methuen. Moi gives a clear, forceful theoretical underpinning which she claims feminist criticism needs.

Re-reading Patriarchy

Eva Figes, <u>Patriarchal Attitudes</u> 1970, See chapter on Figes.

Germaine Greer, <u>The Female Eunuch</u> 1970, Greer is still powerful.

Kate Millett, <u>Sexual Politics</u> 1970, Millett packs her punches.

(The term patriarchy has been problematised in recent criticism.)

Reading/Writing like a Woman

(These terms are listed chronologically, as there is a progress in the approaches in 'Images of Women' in Anglo American criticism

further reading

Patricia Meyer Spacks, The Female Imagination 1975, New York. Spacks bases her articles on perceptive discussions with students about this vast and problematic topic. Today she is criticised for revealing a white middle-class bias, but she is worth reading on the nineteenth-century.

Ellen Moers, Literary Women: The Great Writers 1976, Doubleday N.Y. 1977, Women's Press. Moers surveys nineteenth-century novelists, brilliantly.

Elaine Showalter, A Literature of Their Own: British Women Novelists from Bronte to Lessing 1977, Princeton Univ. Press. 1978, Virago. Epochmaking.

Judith Fetterley, The Resisting Reader: Feminist Approaches to American Fiction 1978, Indiana Univ. Press. This is a valuable re-read.

Sandra M. Gilbert, and Susan Gubar, The Madwoman in the Attic: The Woman Writer and the Nineteenth Century Literary Imagination 1979, Yale Univ. This is an exciting study which does not exclude Jane Austen or George Eliot, though it highlights implicit angers and frustrations.

Mary Jacobus, ed. Women Writing and Writing about Women 1979, Croom Helm.

Elizabeth Abel, ed. Writing and Sexual Difference 1982, Harvester. Abel includes some illuminating but demanding theorists.

Sue Roe, Sue, ed. Women Reading Women's Writing 1987, Harvester.

FEMINISM

Michele Barrett, Women's Oppression Today 1980, provides a forceful introductory account.

Rosalind Brunt, and Caroline Rowan, Feminism, Culture and Politics 1982, Lawrence and Wishart. They present an exceedingly useful range of essays, including Barrett 'A Definition of Cultural Politics'.

Deborah Cameron, Feminism and Linguistic Theory 1985, Macmillan. The clearest comprehensive survey of the strengths (and weaknesses) of present theoretical positions, written with common sense and revolutionary vision.

Hester Hisenstein, <u>Contemporary Feminist Thought</u> 1985, Unwin paperbacks. A wide ranging account of differing historical, social and literary attitudes.

Carolyn Heilbrun, <u>Toward a Recognition of Androgyny</u> 1973, (Harper Colophon Books N.Y., 1974). This is a valuable analysis, and a necessary adjunct to feminist enquiry.

Casey Miller and Kate Swift, <u>Words and Women</u> 1979, Pelican. They present a useful analysis of discrimination in the language of educational books.

Juliet Mitchell, <u>Psychoanalysis and Feminism</u> 1976, Harmondsworth. Mitchell is one of the leading British feminists to use psychoanalysis.

Ann Oakley, <u>Sex, Gender and Society</u> 1972, offers helpful distinctions.

Dale Spender writes clearly and prolifically, but untheoretically. Her epochmaking book was: <u>Man Made Language</u> 1980 Routledge and Kegan Paul. Spender analyses patriarchal discrimination in everyday language, with many cogent examples. <u>Women of Ideas</u> 1985 Ark paperbacks, presents summaries of often neglected women writers and thinkers from Aphra Benn to the present day.
<u>For the Record: The making and meaning of feminist knowledge</u> 1985, The Women's Press. Spender offers accounts of ideas from Friedan onwards. <u>Mothers of the Novel</u> 1986, Pandora. Spender describes the lives of 100 women novelists before Jane Austen, but too little analysis of their books.

Janet Radcliffe Richards, <u>The Sceptical Feminist</u> 1983, Penguin. This presents a sensible critique of a few exaggerated claims.

<u>The Feminist Review</u> contains many relevant articles. It is published three times a year by a collective, 65, Manor Road, London N16.

Three excellent women critics who use contemporary theory:

Gillian Beer, <u>Romance</u> 1970, Methuen. From the Middle Ages to the twenties.

Juliann E. Fleenor, <u>The Female Gothic</u> 1983, Eden Press, Canada.

Rosemary Jackson, <u>Fantasy: The Literature of Subversion</u> 1983, Methuen.